Evaluative Studies

AMERICA'S HOUSING PROBLEM

An approach to its solution

Irving H. Welfeld

With a foreword by George Romney

AMERICA'S
HOUSING PROBLEM

Evaluative Studies

This series of studies seeks to bring about greater understanding and promote continuing review of the activities and functions of the federal government. Each study focuses on a specific program, evaluating its cost and efficiency, the extent to which it achieves its objectives, and the major alternative means—public and private—for reaching those objectives. Yale Brozen, professor of economics at the University of Chicago and an adjunct scholar of the American Enterprise Institute for Public Policy Research, is the director of the program.

AMERICA'S HOUSING PROBLEM

An approach to its solution

Irving H. Welfeld

With a foreword by George Romney

American Enterprise Institute for Public Policy Research
Washington, D. C.

Irving Welfeld is an analyst in the office of the assistant secretary for policy development and research, Department of Housing and Urban Development. The views expressed in this study are his own.

Evaluative Studies 10, October 1973

ISBN 0-8447-3111-0

Library of Congress Catalog Card No. L.C. 73-87585

Printed in the United States of America

Dedicated to the memory of

Morris Welfeld

who was not as wise as his son
in his selection of parents.

What stands most in the way of solving our important problems is the feeling of well-intentioned people that there are no alternatives; all we can do is try to improve present methods.

Paul Goodman

CONTENTS

TABLES

FOREWORD

In the fields of housing and urban or rural development, we face a set of critical issues unmatched for complexity in any other domestic problem area. Particularly acute are the problems of public responsibility for ensuring that low and moderate income families have access to decent housing.

The past decade's efforts to solve these problems have produced important gains. But they have also resulted in approaches that have been mistaken, counterproductive, and unbelievably wasteful of taxpayers' money.

During my term as Secretary of the Department of Housing and Urban Development, I was assisted by a number of thoughtful, searching analysts of urban problems. Among the most helpful was Mr. Irving Welfeld, who served in the Office of the Deputy Under Secretary for Policy Analysis and Program Evaluation.

In my judgment, Mr. Welfeld's monograph on housing, although holding no official status in department policy, either now or in my term of office, makes a major contribution to solving the problems posed by our housing programs. It should have significant impact in the struggle to make necessary reforms.

It is particularly useful that this monograph should appear at a time when the Nixon administration and the Congress are conducting an exhaustive review of the accumulated housing legislation of several decades.

GEORGE ROMNEY
formerly Secretary,
Department of Housing
and Urban Development

1

CHAPTER I

BEGIN AT THE BEGINNING

The basic goal of national housing policy was set forth in the Housing Act of 1949.

> The Congress hereby declares that the general welfare and the security of the Nation and the health and living standards of its people require . . . the realization as soon as feasible of the goal of a decent home and a suitable environment for every American family. . . .[1]

To accomplish this goal, two things must be done. First, there must be enough housing units so that decent housing exists for every family. If there are not enough units, it will be necessary to produce more. Second, every household must be able to afford decent housing. If this is not the case, it will be necessary to provide financial assistance to some households.[2]

Unfortunately, the distinction between housing production and financial assistance has been blurred in the framing of American housing subsidy programs. The basic programs have attempted to solve the "housing problem" by constructing dwelling units for those who cannot afford them. On the production side, the current approach has led to programs that are inefficient, that lack general applicability and market discipline, and that maximize federal involvement, inequity to nonrecipients, and opportunities for fraud. On the assistance side, the current approach has led to programs that serve little more than 10 percent of the households in need of

The author would like to thank Renee Welfeld, John Concannon, Harold C. McKinney and Hilbert Fefferman for their tight reading of the manuscript and their loose rending of criticism.

3

assistance, providing them with excessive amounts of housing services while others as much or more in need receive no assistance.

A new approach is needed—an approach that recognizes the distinction between housing production and financial assistance.

Why Produce Housing?

Even if one accepts the goal of a "decent" home for every American, the necessity for a program of housing production is questionable on two grounds. First, it may be asked—and this is a question of fact—is there a housing shortage? Second, it may be asked—and this is a question of policy—even if there is a housing shortage, would a financial assistance program adequately stimulate increased production without unacceptable side effects?

The Question of Fact. Using as its standard of adequacy the existence of a full complement of plumbing facilities (hot and cold indoor piped water, plus an indoor flush toilet and bathtub or shower for the exclusive use of the unit's occupants), the 1970 Census counted 4,668,303 inadequate, year-round housing units (6.9 percent of the existing stock).[3] Of these, 1,699,682 units were in urban areas and 2,985,539 were in rural areas. Inadequate housing in urban areas represented 3.4 percent of total urban housing units, and inadequate housing in rural areas constituted 16.9 percent of total rural housing units.[4]

In addition to the inadequate units, a sizable number of adequate units were overcrowded.[5] Defining overcrowding as more than 1.5 persons per room, 1,028,291 units were overcrowded.[6] Defining overcrowding as more than 1.0 persons per room, 4,464,376 units were overcrowded. Depending on the definition of overcrowding, the sum of inadequate (those lacking complete facilities) and overcrowded adequate units was either 9.1 or 5.7 million units in 1969.

This does not imply that the goal of adequate housing cannot be accomplished by private enterprise without a federal presence. Since the passage of the Housing Act of 1949, housing production has far outpaced new household formation. Over the twenty-year period from 1950 through 1970, approximately 1.5 new housing units were constructed for each new household formed despite the even more rapid growth in households than in population. (The median size of households declined from 3.1 to 2.7 persons during this period.) Inadequate housing (units lacking a full complement of plumbing facilities) dropped from 37 percent of the housing stock in 1950 to 17 percent in 1960 to 7 percent in 1970. The incidence of overcrowding (more than one person per room) dropped from 16 percent in 1950 to 12 percent in 1960 to 8 percent in 1970.[7]

This, indeed, occurred during a period when the net effect of government action on the housing stock was negative—that is, government programs destroyed more units than they built.[8] The main causes of the housing improvement were (1) the productivity of private enterprise in building and rehabilitating and (2) the federal bulldozer, insofar as it demolished (through the urban renewal, public housing and highway programs) more substandard than standard units.

Only within the last five years has federally subsidized construction been significant. Housing produced under federal programs totaled 163,360 units in 1968, increased to 430,990 units in 1970, 433,480 in 1971 and an estimated 452,300 in 1972.[9] This level of federal activity need not be an enduring feature of the housing scene since the basic problem is not the private sector's inability to produce an adequate supply of decent housing. The problem is not on the supply side but on the demand side.

A Question of Policy. Even with the present shortage of decent units, the need for a direct federal presence in production is not self-evident. Why not attempt to kill two birds with one stone? If housing allowances were given to poor families, would not these families be able to pay for standard units? In response to the increase in demand, would not suppliers produce more units?

There are at least five possible scenarios for an assistance program which (1) increases the number of poor households covered and (2) provides payments at a level sufficient to permit the poor to bid for higher quality housing but is not so generous as to enable them to afford new housing.

1. The poor outbid lower middle-income households for standard units. The latter move into the units vacated by the poor.

2. The poor do not outbid lower middle-income households for standard units and remain residents of their original units.

3. Either (1) or (2) is the case and landlords raise prices on the units originally occupied by the poor.

4. Either (1) or (2) is the case and landlords raise prices on the units originally occupied by the poor but also improve their quality.

5. The poor pay more and obtain the standard apartments of lower middle-income households. The latter in turn pay more [10] and obtain better housing. This ripple effect ends when builders add to the housing supply inasmuch as the price of the new units is competitive with the rent of older units.

The scenarios are simplified. It is likely that the actual result of the assistance program defined above might be some combination of the third, fourth and fifth scenarios. However, it is clear that the possibility that some nonpoor households end up in poorer housing or suffer higher housing costs reduces the attractiveness of a housing policy that relies exclusively on assistance.

Why Give Financial Assistance?

A government housing production strategy would move in the opposite direction from a strategy of financial assistance. With an increase in the supply of housing, the ripple effect (more commonly referred to as the filtering or turnover process) would tend to lower housing costs to lower income households in relative if not absolute terms. If this in fact were the result of a production program, would a program of financial assistance be necessary? As production was increased to a level where the housing gap is closed, would not the housing problem of the poor be solved?

Based on the evidence of the recent past, the answer to the last question is no. Increases in the number of units and decreases in population during the past twenty years have substantially improved the housing situation of the poor in central cities. In this regard middle class blight is often the same phenomenon as an increase in housing opportunities for lower class families. Nevertheless, despite the improvement in the supply situation for the poor, the price of standard, uncrowded, unsubsidized housing to a poor family is high relative to its income, leaving little for other necessities.

In 1970, the median rent/income ratio in the United States, for renter households with incomes of less than $5,000, was 35 percent.[11] This compares with a median rent/income ratio of 18.9 percent for households with incomes between $5,000 and $9,999, of 13.9 percent for households with incomes between $10,000 and $14,999, and 10.7 percent for households with incomes of $15,000 or more.[12]

Table 1, which sets forth income and expense data for low-income families in fifty-five areas in fifty-one of the nation's largest cities, illustrates the housing problem still facing the poor living in private housing. The first column shows the median payment made by poor families for private housing. (Poor families are those with incomes below the Social Security Administration's poverty yard-sticks. In 1969, the poverty cutoff for a nonfarm family of four, a typical size in poor urban neighborhoods, was $3,880.)[13] For renter-households, the payment shown is rent plus all utilities. For

Table 1

THE PRICE THE POOR PAY FOR HOUSING

		Median Monthly Housing Expense of Poor Families[a]	Median Annual Family Income of Working Poor[b]	Rent/ Income Ratio
1	New York—All	$ 90	$3,100	35%
2	Manhattan	89	2,900	37
3	Brooklyn	83	3,200	31
4	Bronx	90	3,200	34
5	Queens	131	2,200	71
6	Los Angeles	90	3,200	34
7	Chicago	115	2,000	69
8	Philadelphia	74	2,600	34
9	Detroit	88	1,600	66
10	San Francisco	120	2,100	69
11	Washington, D. C.	115	3,800	36
12	Boston	109	2,000	65
13	Pittsburgh	65	3,100	25
14	St. Louis	74	2,200	40
15	Baltimore, Md.	94	2,400	47
16	Cleveland	87	2,800	45
17	Houston	80	3,000	32
18	Newark	114	2,100	65
19	Dallas	89	2,800	38
20	Minneapolis	110	3,900	34
21	St. Paul	92	2,500	44
22	Milwaukee	88	2,800	38
23	Atlanta	75	2,500	36
24	Cincinnati	78	2,400	39
25	Buffalo	71	3,100	27
26	San Diego	87	2,900	36
27	Miami, Fla.	106	2,600	49
28	Kansas City, Mo.	76	2,600	35
29	Denver	81	3,100	31
30	Indianapolis	80	3,000	32
31	New Orleans	74	2,900	31
32	Oakland, Calif.	94	2,600	43
33	Tampa, Fla.	62	3,200	23
34	Portland, Oreg.	76	1,700	54
35	Phoenix, Ariz.	66	3,500	23
36	Columbus, Ohio	76	2,600	35
37	San Antonio, Tex.	40	3,600	13
38	Dayton, Ohio	69	2,700	31
39	Rochester, N. Y.	98	3,500	34
40	Louisville, Ky.	63	2,500	30
41	Memphis, Tenn.	59	3,100	23
42	Fort Worth, Tex.	63	3,200	24
43	Birmingham, Ala.	42	2,800	18
44	Toledo, Ohio	76	1,900	48
45	Akron, Ohio	84	1,900	53
46	Norfolk, Va.	71	3,200	27
47	Oklahoma City, Okla.	63	3,300	23
48	Jersey City, N. J.	92	2,500	44
49	Providence, R. I.	72	3,100	28

Table 1 (continued)

THE PRICE THE POOR PAY FOR HOUSING

		Median Monthly Housing Expense of Poor Families[a]	Median Annual Family Income of Working Poor[b]	Rent Income Ratio
50	Omaha, Nebr.	$ 79	$2,200	43%
51	Youngstown, Ohio	66	2,400	33
52	Tulsa, Okla.	63	2,900	26
53	Charlotte, N. C.	70	3,000	28
54	Wichita, Kans.	66	4,100	19
55	Bridgeport, Conn.	117	4,000	35
	Urban Summary	83	2,900	34

[a] Mortgage payment or rent plus utilities.

[b] Full time (35 hours a week, 50 weeks a year); does not include supplementary income in kind such as food stamps, free lunches, Medicaid, and housing subsidies.

Source: Derived by John Concannon and author from U.S. Bureau of the Census, *Employment Profiles of Selected Low Income Areas: Reports (1-60)* (Washington: U.S. Government Printing Office, 1972).

owner-households, the amount is the mortgage payment plus all utilities. The second column shows the average total income of a poor family the head of which works full time (more than thirty-five hours a week, fifty weeks a year). The third column shows the rent/income ratio of these poor families assuming that average income of those in private housing is the same as the average income of all the full-time working poor in the area. In almost all of the fifty-five areas the ratio is high (although somewhat overstated for reasons indicated in footnote b, Table 1). In Newark, San Francisco, Detroit, Chicago, Boston and parts of New York City, it is very high—over 60 percent.

Of course, not all poor families pay such a high relative price for their housing. But when they do not, the housing stock and the neighborhood suffer. Elderly homeowners who scrimp by saving on maintenance are milking their property in the same way as the proverbial slum landlord (who often turns out to be an elderly widow) and have the same effect on the housing stock. The poor families who default on their FHA-insured mortgages are behaving in the same manner as the managers of public housing units who find themselves unable even to cover their operating costs. In this way much of the production effort to increase the supply of housing is undercut.

As a result of increases in supply, standard housing "filters down." But, if poor households cannot (or will not) pay the amounts necessary to cover the basic expenses of ownership and operation, housing will "filter out" through disinvestment and abandonment. This is illustrated not only by the abandonment of private housing in the central cities, but also by the massive disinvestment through deferred maintenance by local housing authorities (LHAs). Thus, without a program of financial assistance, the gains brought about by increased production are offset by a lack of effective demand.

The Political Answer. If assistance is necessary, the obvious economic question is why should it be given in the form of housing dollars rather than cash? Would not the taxpayer and the family be far better off with unrestricted direct cash payments? Would not a single cash payment be a more efficient way of dispensing welfare than a series of separate programs? Would not the poor family have greater freedom and dignity if it were allowed to decide how to spend the money?

The obvious practical answer is that the unrestricted cash payment is not popular with voters. After a four-year effort, the family assistance plan, which embodies a $2,400 minimum for a family of four, went down to defeat under a hail of criticism from left and right. The $2,400 minimum was both too low (for people unable to work) and too high (for people unwilling to work). Depending on one's political perspective, the family assistance plan represented a giant leap forward, or a long step backward, from the present "unworkable and undesirable" welfare system.[14] In either case, it was politically unfeasible.

There are political advantages to restricting the cash transfer to specified essentials. As James Tobin has written, "The social conscience is more offended by severe inequality in nutrition, and basic shelter . . . than by inequality in automobiles, books, clothes, furniture. . . ."[15] Even from a purely economic point of view, restricted transfers may have advantages when viewed within a broadened analytical framework. As Roger Scott has written in a recent article:

> I have taught my students that such taxes and subsidies were "economically inefficient." Now, suddenly, I fear I may have been mistaken. For the world of interdependence forces me to recognize that the framework for analysis of economic inefficiency that I once used ignored an important systematic interdependence of utilities.
>
> If a starving moron freely spends his money on balloons instead of food, who am I to say he is irrational in his behavior? I am forced to presume that his happiness is best served by his "revealed preference." But if I am to be asked to help pay for his care, then should my preferences have no weight in deciding what he will consume?[16]

CHAPTER II

ASSESSMENT OF EXISTING PROGRAMS

Policy Criteria

A decision regarding a basic structure for the subsidy system is only the first step. With the basic structure set, it is still necessary to determine the specific programs. We must look at the criteria for judging the efficaciousness and efficiency of housing programs and see how fully the existing programs satisfy these criteria.

policy criteria

Housing Production. A well-designed production program must, in the author's view, satisfy tests on performance, efficiency, general applicability, effective incentives, reduction of federal presence, consumer choice, minimized opportunity for fraud, and minimum inequity.

Performance. The program should be capable of enticing builders and landlords to construct and upgrade more units than would have been built or rehabilitated in its absence. It should not result simply in substituting the production of subsidized units for units which would have been built with no subsidy.

Efficiency. The program should result in the production of housing services at a low cost to the taxpayer.

General applicability. The program should be operable in all areas of the country and should take into account regional differences in incomes and housing costs.

Effective incentives. The program should not enable a profit to be reaped if housing is built where no need exists or is below par in terms of location, structural quality or price. The subsidy should not bail out a poor builder or manager.

Reduction of federal presence. The program should require no more than a minimum of governmental regulation and supervision. This criterion is closely related to the effective incentive criterion. To the extent incentives are effective, the direct government role can be reduced. Much of the paper work, processing, and regulation in federal housing programs results from the absence of effective incentives. When it turned out in the late 1940s that developers could obtain large profits by building rental projects which had to be repossessed by the FHA because of the lack of tenants, the ensuing scandal brought administrative requirements that are now criticized as bureaucracy and red tape. The paper work and supervision often amount to an administrative patchwork on a surface undermined by structural defects.

Consumer choice. The program should offer a choice in price, building type, unit size and location.

Minimized opportunity for fraud. The program should not provide a few developers and builders with the equivalent of a grant of hunting privileges in a game preserve. When a subsidy allocation becomes a bounty rather than a license, it also becomes an invitation to corrupt the gamekeeper.

Minimized inequity. There are three aspects to this problem. The program should minimize unfairness between the beneficiary and his economic peers, between the beneficiary and those above him on the economic totem pole, and between the beneficiary and those below him in economic level.

Although traces of unfairness will always be present in any nonuniversal subsidy, there are, nevertheless, ways to minimize its extent and intensity. If the opportunity to benefit is available to all and the selection process is fair, the pain may be no worse than the pain of "losing" a lottery that an economic equal has "won." If the subsidy enables the recipient to obtain better housing but at a greater effort (a higher rent/income ratio) than a household with higher income, the higher income household may overlook the recipient's good luck. If the subsidy assists the higher income household to acquire new housing, any sting of unfairness to those lower on the totem pole can be salved if there is also a benefit to them in the form of increased housing opportunities—that is, if they can move into the house from which the higher income family moved.

Financial Assistance. With differences where appropriate, the criteria for a well-designed assistance program are like those listed above:

Performance. The program should enable every poor household to pay the price of decent housing.

Efficiency. The program should produce this result at minimum expense to the taxpayer with minimum impact on the cost of housing to others.

General applicability. The program should be operable in all areas of the country and should take into account regional differences in incomes and housing costs.

Effective incentives. The program should reward the landlord who meets the housing demands and needs of the poor. The program should not entice the consumer to pay such a high percentage of his income that he has little left for necessities nor entrap a poor family (by requiring only a nominal investment) into purchasing a home it is unable to maintain.

Minimized federal presence. The program should require no more than a minimum of federal regulation and supervision.

Consumer choice. The program should offer a choice in price, building type, unit size, and location.

Minimized opportunity for fraud. The program should put the barrier of self-interest in the path of those who would be tempted to fraud.

Minimized inequity. The benefits of the program should be available to all poor households. The program should not enable a lower income household to obtain a more expensive unit than a higher income household unless the lower income household tries harder (has a higher rent/income ratio).

Evaluation of Existing Programs

Are new programs necessary if national housing goals are to be achieved? Many claim that the existing programs are basically sound, but that better management or more funds are needed. To examine this claim it is necessary (1) to describe the programs and evaluate them against the policy criteria given above and then (2) to assess whether program deficiencies are the result of the design, management, or levels of funding. To the extent that each program combines production of housing and financial assistance, each program will be evaluated against both sets of criteria.

Public Housing.[1] Enacted in 1937, this program is designed to provide new and substantially rehabilitated rental units at below market rents for low-income households. The housing is developed, owned, and administered by local housing authorities. The LHAs finance projects through the sale of tax-exempt bonds to private investors. The federal government makes annual subsidy payments in sufficient amounts so that a project's rent needs only to cover the expenses of operation, repair and maintenance, plus payments in lieu of local taxes. These payments are set equal to 10 percent of the shelter rent (rents received less utilities). Where the rent required to meet these costs would exceed 25 percent of a tenant's income, the federal government also subsidizes maintenance costs.

Eligibility for residence in a project is in general limited to families in the lowest income group (as defined by the LHAs), including low-income households that are either elderly (which includes the handicapped and disabled) or displaced.

Performance and efficiency: production. The public housing program has induced builders to construct more low-rent units than they otherwise would. In the absence of the program, no builder could construct units at a low enough rent to enable the income group served to afford them. As of the end of 1971, 950,000 public housing units were under management and an additional 117,000 units were in various stages of construction.[2]

As a matter of basic economic logic, public housing, in attempting to assist poor households by producing *new* units, has to be a highly inefficient instrument. Given the total amount of government assistance and given a fixed cost per unit because the amount of housing provided does not vary with income, the result is that the poorer the families assisted the fewer the families that are assisted. This occurs because of the following circumstances:

(1) The number of units that can be subsidized varies inversely with the size of the average unit subsidy. For example, assuming $10,000 is available for subsidies, a $1,000 per unit payment will support ten units. A $2,000 payment will support only five units.

(2) The amount of the subsidy payment needed varies inversely with the rent that a unit's occupant pays. To illustrate, for an apartment renting at $2,500 per annum, if the occupant is required to pay $1,500, the needed subsidy is $1,000; if he pays only $500, the need is for $2,000.

(3) The amount of rent an occupant is required to pay varies directly with his income. If one assumes a fixed 20 percent rent/income ratio, a person making $7,500 pays $1,500. A person making $2,500 pays $500.

(4) The lower the incomes of the occupants selected, the higher the amount of the subsidy payment per unit. The total number of units which can be subsidized is reduced.

The actual numbers demonstrate the validity of the logic. In practice today, the annual debt service contribution necessary for new units is over $1,500, and annual operating subsidies are approaching $500 per unit. In addition, there is a federal revenue expenditure of approximately $300 per unit resulting from the financing of the project through tax-exempt bonds, as well as a local contribution, since the payment in lieu of taxes is substantially less than would otherwise be paid. It adds up to an annual subsidy of approximately $2,400 annually for each unit for forty years.[3]

Performance and efficiency: assistance. The public housing program has enabled some poor households to afford the cost of decent units. However, all of the large housing authorities are on their fiscal knees begging the federal government for very large sums of money. The LHAs seem to be more in need of a trustee in bankruptcy than of additional beneficiaries.

To some extent the fiscal problems are a result of the Brooke amendments. This legislation reduced the income of housing authorities by setting a maximum rent/income ratio of 25 percent and by redefining income to exclude (1) nonrecurring income, (2) $300 for each dependent and $300 for each secondary wage earner, (3) 5 percent of gross income (10 percent in the case of the elderly), and (4) extraordinary medical expenses. The most recent Brooke amendment enacted in December of 1971 prohibited states and localities from reducing welfare benefits if application of the 25 percent limitation reduced rents to the tenants. All welfare recipients in public housing are now eligible for rent reductions. The loss in shelter rent as a result of this provision is estimated to be between $60 and $100 million. Although the Brooke amendments may be the provisions that broke the program's back, public housing was already chronically ill. Albert Walsh, writing in 1969, put the issue starkly: "The question—'Is Public Housing Heading for a Fiscal Crisis?'— must have been framed solely for the sake of rhetoric. Let there be no doubt about it: public housing is not heading for a fiscal crisis; it is already in a fiscal crisis. The only question is what will be done about it."[4] And in April 1969, the Department of Housing and Urban Development (HUD) supplied the House Appropriations Committee with the following grim picture:

> The 15 major-sized local housing authorities with financial problems are: Washington, D.C., Kansas City, Mo., San Francisco, California, St. Louis, Mo., Columbus, Ohio, New York City, New Haven, Conn., Omaha, Nebr., Boston, Mass., Newark, N.J., Chicago, Ill., Los Angeles, Calif., Philadelphia, Pa., Louisville, Ky., and Detroit, Michigan. . . .
>
> The greatest contributing factor is the fact that total operating costs in line with the economy in general have

increased at a greater rate than has project income. Several factors have contributed to the lower rate of increase in project income with the most basic being that the low-rent program has . . . housed a progressively large proportion of the lowest income group.[5]

The benefit received by poor households from the public housing program is not commensurate with its cost to the taxpayer. The 1969 subsidy for new units, not taking into account the tenant's rent, is approximately twice the amount of the 1969 median rent in the United States. Public housing tenants are being provided with units which cost approximately two-and-one-half times the average cost of housing occupied by the taxpaying public.

General applicability. The program has operated in all major geographical regions of the country. Nevertheless, the distribution of public housing units has been quite uneven.[6]

Effective incentives. Incentives for controlling construction costs are absent from the program. As long as the federal subsidy picks up the full cost of the debt service, the local housing authority has no real stake in lowering costs.[7]

Incentives for effective management have also been totally absent from the program. In prior years, "profits" arising out of a project's operations were returned to the federal government, so that some of the tenants' rental payments reduced the federal subsidy for amortization. In recent years, federal operating subsidies have been granted (in addition to amortization subsidies) to make up the deficit between rental income and operating costs. These latter subsidies are only paid, however, if the LHA lacks reserves—a thrifty federal policy that rewards the prodigal LHA.

Reduced federal presence. The public housing situation is a case of achieving the worst of both worlds—detailed federal supervision for generations accompanied by a minimal amount of leverage. Federal handbooks, reviews, and audits attempt to guide, control, and check the design, production, utilization and management of public housing. Nevertheless, federal control over the cost seems to be declining. As former Secretary George Romney of the Department of Housing and Urban Development told the House Appropriations Committee in the spring of 1972:

> The basic authority for the operation of these public housing projects is in the hands of the local housing authorities, and the Federal government has in effect said: "We are going to guarantee what your costs are, including your operating costs." Now, this Department has a very restricted and limited means of undertaking to see that these operations are as economical and as efficient as they ought

to be and that is the budget review. Except for that, we have no means of seeing that this is wisely done. . . .[8]

Consumer choice. The location, the design limitations, the concentration of low-income families, and the increasing nonwhite occupancy of public housing have resulted in a product that is often of limited appeal to the poor. E. D. Huttman has written:

> Public housing is perceived as an unhappy, stigmatized environment by tenants and public alike. To the tenant, it is a stressful environment created by poor management policies, the unacceptable actions of other tenants, the isolation and size of the projects, and socially unpleasant aspects of the housing design itself. To a large proportion of the public today, it is viewed negatively as a government repository for socially unfit families. *Ironically, a public effort to build decent housing for the poor has produced housing whose reputation is worse than that of the slums.* [Emphasis added.] [9]

Nevertheless, in spite of all its deficiencies, public housing is most likely to be the only housing subsidy game in town that the poor can afford.

Minimized opportunity for fraud. The absence of profit possibility and motive for the LHA, as owner, makes its interest in monetary gain from good management as strong as the eunuch's interest in sex. That, however, does not eliminate the possibility of hanky panky in the harem. Since much of the construction process is in the hands of private developers, the danger of fraud always exists. This danger is heightened by the fact that when we are dealing with everybody's money we are dealing with nobody's money. As a result, rules and regulations guide the entire development process to such a degree that the overall increase in the average costs of public housing is sufficient to finance the good life for a squadron of thieves.

The history of the Turnkey program is illustrative of this phenomenon. As originally conceived and operated there was little regulation of the developer. The initial experience resulted both in units far cheaper than conventionally produced and in a number of scandals. Regulations were imposed and the development process was made so much more complex that the Turnkey method is now more expensive than LHA designed and managed construction.

Minimized inequity. The households that pay the price for the inefficiency and ineffectiveness of public housing are not only the taxpayers but also the poor themselves. After thirty-six years, the odds that a poor household will be accommodated in public housing are sixteen to one. For public policy to enable the "fortunate few" to live in *new* public housing units (even if the quality of the units were commensurate with their cost) is misguided generosity, comparable to a food program that allowed a select few of the poor to dine in expensive restaurants while the rest were left to fend for themselves.

Section 221(d)(3)—the Rent Supplement Program.[10] Enacted in 1965, this program is designed to provide new and substantially rehabilitated rental units for low-income households. The housing is developed by private builders. Projects are financed through private lending institutions and the mortgages are insured by the Federal Housing Administration (FHA), primarily under Section 221(d)(3), at a market interest rate. The FHA pays rent supplements to the landlord to cover the difference between a unit's rent and an amount equal to 25 percent of the occupant's adjusted income (but the supplement may not exceed 70 percent of the rent). Ownership of the project is limited to nonprofit sponsors and others willing to limit their profit to 6 percent of 11 percent of the mortgage (6 percent of a presumed 10 percent equity).

Eligibility for the program is limited to families and individuals whose income at the time of initial occupancy is at or below public housing income limits for admission and who are elderly, handicapped, displaced by government action, victims of disaster, or living in substandard housing.

The similarity of the rent supplement program to the public housing program makes a point-by-point comparison unnecessary. The reliance on private rather than public entrepreneurs does not change the basic economic illogic inherent in producing new units for poor people.[11] Nor has it resulted in high volume production. Since 1968, the program has produced an average of 16,000 units a year.[12]

There is an apparent major difference between public housing and rent supplements. The estimated annual subsidy for new units in the rent supplement program is approximately $1,500, substantially less than the $2,400 needed for public housing. However, there is less to this cost differential than meets the eye.

The market-rate rent supplement program is only operable in low-cost areas. Because of its rent and cost limits, new units cannot be financed under the basic program in most metropolitan areas in the North and West. Thus, in high-cost areas, the rent supplement program is generally hitched to another program. In the usual case, a project is financed under Section 236, which involves an interest

18

subsidy of approximately $1,000, and the rent supplement subsidy is then piggybacked on top of the Section 236 interest subsidy. Since many of these projects are also receiving real estate tax abatements and are located on land that benefited from urban renewal write-downs, costs per unit are comparable to those under public housing in high cost areas. Otherwise the program would not be operable in those areas.

Section 235—the Homeownership Program.[13] This program is designed to enable "lower income" households to purchase homes. It was enacted as part of the Housing and Urban Development Act of 1968. Under the program, most of the housing has been new and has been developed by private builders. Projects are financed through private lending institutions, and the mortgages are insured by the FHA at a market interest rate. HUD makes interest subsidy payments to the mortgagee in an amount sufficient to cover the difference between the total costs of debt service, taxes, insurance, and mortgage insurance, and a figure equal to 20 percent of the household's adjusted income. The maximum amount of the subsidy payment is the difference between the cost of debt service at the market rate of interest (plus the mortgage insurance premium) and, at 1 percent. An eligible "lower income" household is one whose income is not in excess of 135 percent of the local public housing limit for initial occupancy (taking into account the size of the household).

Performance. In producing housing, the Section 235 interest subsidy program has been a spectacular success compared to previous federal efforts. Since 1968, 400,000 units have been produced under the program,[14] compared to a total of 200,000 units built under earlier subsidy programs between 1935 and 1949 and to 410,000 units built during the fifties.[15] But as a vehicle for financial assistance for the poor, Section 235 has been a failure. The typical income of a four-person family in the program in 1972 was over $6,300.[16] Fewer than 4 percent of the households entering the program in that year had incomes under $4,000.[17]

Efficiency. As a vehicle for producing housing, the program is relatively efficient. The typical annual subsidy in 1971 was approximately $960 per unit,[18] a small sum compared to public housing or rent supplement subsidies. The comparison is even more favorable if we accept the assumption that the household will work its way off the subsidy so that the total cost will be approximately $9,000.[19] As a vehicle for assistance, Section 235 can only be justified on the basis that the households directly served by the program cannot afford new housing. Wallace Smith has summarized and demolished this justification:

> Housing commentators in the United States are fond of producing data which show that new housing is priced beyond the means of most of the middle-income population as well as the low-income group. *It is a non sequitur to conclude that middle-income households require housing subsidies, because this group finds its housing primarily in the existing stock of dwellings.* Indeed, the ordinary home-builder's reason for not trying to build homes for the lower-middle income group is that he cannot compete with the used housing market where such families get substantially more for their housing dollar. [Emphasis added.] [20]

General applicability. The mortgage limits of the program are $18,000 for a three-bedroom unit and $21,000 for larger houses— or $21,000 and $24,000, respectively, in high-cost areas. As in the rent supplement program, Section 235 is inoperable in many metropolitan areas in the North and West. Over 50 percent of the insured mortgages are in two of HUD's ten administrative regions, the South and Southwest. [21]

Effective incentives. The program's incentives push toward a higher priced house. Since the subsidy amount is based on debt service (the statutory formula is the lesser of (1) the difference between debt service at the market rate of interest and at 1 percent, or (2) the difference between (a) debt service, taxes, insurance, and mortgage insurance and (b) 20 percent of the household's adjusted income), the highest subsidies are paid for the families that can afford the most expensive houses. Since a higher priced unit brings a greater profit, the builder is happy to oblige. [22] To cite a hypothetical example taken from material HUD submitted to Congress in 1970, [23] a family with an income of $8,000 pays the same amount, $116.67 a month, whether it purchases a house with a $14,000 or a $25,000 mortgage. The only difference is that the monthly subsidy is $11.67 in the case of the $14,000 mortgage and $121.20 in the case of the $25,000 mortgage.

By December of 1972, the program reached the stage where the entire country was a high cost area. During the month of December, the average mortgage on a new unit was $19,354. The average for the traditionally low cost southern region was over $18,000. [24]

There are real luxury elements in the program. As many as 50 percent of the households in the program are being overhoused relative to the national average and, therefore, oversubsidized. Approximately 50 percent of the families entering the Section 235 program would only qualify for a two bedroom apartment under most of HUD's multifamily housing programs.[25] Nevertheless, virtually all of the homes in this program have three or more bedrooms.

In addition to the fact that Section 235's subsidy costs are higher than necessary, units are being produced in some areas in spite of a surplus of standard units available in the market. It would require a major depression before it would become difficult to sell new homes whose carrying costs are 35 percent below the cost of equivalent new housing. What buyer will settle for a $14,000 used house when his monthly costs on that house will exceed those on a new $18,000 subsidized unit? The irony of this situation is that HUD is often being hoist on its own petard. The success of the Section 235 program is often accompanied by a rising inventory of foreclosed homes.

Minimized federal presence. The Section 235 program is a prime example of a case where increased federal involvement is of no avail in overcoming structural faults in a program. There is in fact a high correlation between insufferable paper work and insoluble problems. It became apparent fairly early in the program that the cost of the new units was rising sharply. In calendar 1969, the median mortgage amount for new units was $15,544. In the first quarter of 1970 it rose to $16,133. Nevertheless, in spite of memoranda to regional and district officials imploring them to keep costs down, the trend has continued upward. It rose to $17,341 for calendar year 1970 and to $17,951 in calendar year 1971. By the end of 1972 the cumulative total was $18,252. The suspicion spread in Washington that local officials were either illiterate or incompetent. This suspicion overlooked the fact that it is to no one's interest to build a cheap unit— no one's except, of course, the taxpayer's.

HUD also faced a problem with respect to existing units which were mortgaged to low-income households in inner city areas. Many of the households defaulted when they could not meet both mortgage payments and unexpected maintenance costs. The program, to the extent that it provides ownership opportunities to marginal mortgagors in marginal neighborhoods, has deficiencies that cannot be overcome by administration no matter how skillful. There is no way (except through increased subsidy) to avoid exposing the homeowner to the danger of unexpected major catastrophes without pricing the buyer out of the market initially. Adopting a metaphor from the automobile market, it may be said that this aspect of the program dealt with low-income buyers who could not afford the new Ford "Pinto." The program offered lower priced six-year-old Mercury "Marauders." In the Section 235 program, as in the used car business, the trade-off was between lower debt service and higher maintenance costs.

Consumer choice. Section 235 is the first major U.S. housing subsidy program designed to permit the family to purchase rather than rent. The typical family in the program has sufficient income to purchase an existing house, but the program provides such a family with an opportunity to purchase a new and more expensive home. The median cost of the new homes purchased under Section 235 in 1972 was approximately $18,500.[26] The median value of existing homes in areas in which the program is popular is lower. In South Carolina, for example, it is $13,000, in Texas $12,000.[27]

Minimized opportunity for fraud. The Section 235 commitment is a valuable piece of paper for the developer. These commitments reduce the price (in terms of monthly debt service payments) to approximately 35 percent below market value. Since to most home buyers the crucial number is the monthly payment rather than the sales price, a builder can find customers for his unit even if it is worth less than the sales price. When the value of the commitment is coupled with a large amount of administrative discretion in its allocation, the conditions that foster spontaneous corruption have been created.

The channeling of the subsidy commitments through builders and brokers rather than buyers has also permitted the preemption of a sizeable portion of the benefits of the program and maximized the opportunities for fraud. Twenty-four percent of the new houses and 39 percent of the existing homes in a random sample of homes inspected by HUD's Office of Audit either had defects resulting from poor workmanship or materials or significant defects affecting safety, health, or livability.[28]

Minimized inequity. The equity problem in the Section 235 program is threefold, centering among those poorer than program beneficiaries, the peers of program beneficiaries, and those higher on the ladder than the beneficiaries. Complaints are coming in from all sides. The first source of discontent is the family that is the program's intended beneficiary—but does not benefit—the household with income between $3,500 and $5,000. The cost of the average Section 235 home is above the mortgage limit established for the program in non-high cost areas. In the words of the National Tenant's Organization, it is a "perversion of subsidies from the neediest families." [29] The second source of discontent is focused among the economic peers of the program beneficiary. As Secretary Romney noted:

> I don't blame people who are writing in to us and Congressmen, and saying, look, Joe Blow next door makes the same amount of money, he's got the same number of kids. Why

should he get his mortgage interest costs reduced to 1 percent, and I still have to pay 7 and 8 percent? . . .

I don't think you can avoid all inequity, but when it gets to that magnitude, as at present, why, you've got a real problem, and a growing problem, because even if we achieved the national housing goals by 1978, only one fourth of the families eligible for these housing programs will be getting assistance. There will be three complaining like Joe Blow, and only one that's getting the help, and I'm just telling you that isn't politically feasible.[30]

The third source is the family with a higher income, which does not understand why it is taxed to provide a better house, at a lower price, to the man of "lesser worth" next door.

Section 236—the Rental Program.[31] This program is designed to produce new and substantially rehabilitated rental units for "lower income" households. Like the 235 program, it was enacted as part of the Housing and Urban Development Act of 1968. Under Section 236, housing is developed by private builders. Projects are financed through private lending institutions and the mortgages are insured by FHA at a market interest rate. Mortgage interest payments are made to the lender as if the interest rate of the mortgage were equal to 1 percent, and HUD pays the mortgagee the difference between 1 percent and the market rate. Each tenant pays the greater of a basic rental (calculated on the assumption of a mortgage with a 1 percent interest rate) or 25 percent of his adjusted income. Rentals collected by the mortgagor in excess of basic charges are returned to HUD. As in the rent supplement case, ownership is restricted to nonprofit and limited-profit sponsors. Tenant eligibility is the same as it is under the Section 235 program.

Performance. In producing housing, the Section 236 rental program has, like Section 235, been a spectacular success. Since 1968, 365,000 units have been produced under the program[32]—a record matched only by Section 235. But Section 236 has been a failure in providing financial assistance to the poor. According to 1970 HUD cost estimates, in a project with mortgages of $18,000 per unit (an amount close to the average for units constructed in 1972), the subsidized basic monthly rent would be $131.15. For a family with an annual gross income of $4,500, this amount represents 35 percent of income.[33] Tenants with lower incomes threaten the stability of a project because they are unable to cope with rent increases, or do so with great difficulty. Therefore, to protect projects from the poor, HUD has attempted to bar entry to those who would have to pay 35 percent, or more, of their incomes.[34]

Efficiency: Production. As a vehicle for the production of housing, Section 236 has many of the same features as Section 235. The first-year subsidy per unit under the program is approximately the same as under the homeownership program. Although run-out costs are estimated to be between two and three times higher than in the ownership program,[35] this reflects the assumption that home-owners who outgrow the subsidy will continue to occupy their units, but that renters who outgrow the subsidy will also outgrow the apartments—the great bulk of the apartments having two or less bedrooms. If the programs were measured on the basis of number of subsidized families served by a given amount of subsidy, the costs would be similar.

Efficiency: Assistance. As a vehicle for financial assistance, Section 236 involves the same non sequitur as its interest subsidy twin. However, its growth pattern may be very different. At present the program is ill-designed to serve the poor, but in future years its only market may be the poor. This is the result in the main of its requirement that tenants pay a minimum of 25 percent of their income for rent. As long as the units are new and comparable to conventionally financed new apartments, there will be sufficient lower middle-income households willing to pay this percentage of their income in order to obtain a unit at a bargain price. As the units age (the mortgage is for forty years) the admission price will be too high for households with choice. The 25 percent requirement will be attractive only to poor households. In this event, the program may follow the pattern of public housing, which moved from a lower middle and middle-income program in the 1940s to a low-income program in the 1960s. It is not surprising, therefore, that the Senate-passed Housing and Urban Development Act of 1972 provided for operating subsidies in the Section 236 program.[36]

General applicability. Unlike the rent supplement and Section 235 programs, the Section 236 program has worked in all areas of the country.[37] A crucial part of this success may be traced to the tremendous leverage resulting from a very low interest rate. The program's 1 percent interest rate produces a debt service rate (interest plus principal) of 3.33 percent on a forty-year mortgage. Assuming a 90 percent mortgage, this means that each dollar of project net income can support $27 of debt—more than twice the amount that can be supported under a market-rate mortgage. More-over, (1) the "lower income" limits have turned out to be higher than anyone expected. In many cases, they have been close to the median income of the locality. Also (2) HUD has processed applications on the assumption that the occupants of the building would have incomes at a maximum income limit and would be spending 25 percent of their incomes for rent (the latter is a statutory requirement). And generally (3) the developers' "guesstimates" of future operating expenses have been accepted.

Effective incentives. The incentives resulting from combining the federal tax code with the Section 236 program promote inefficiency. What draws developers and investors to subsidized housing is not the 6 percent return, but rather the real estate tax preference, which consists

> primarily of highly favorable tax depreciation, enhanced by thin equity financing and reduced or deferred taxation of gains on the disposition of the investment. These are frequently combined into varying arrangements called the real estate shelter which not only provides tax free cash flow, but may offer syndicated investors an opportunity to apply excess real estate deductions to shelter other income from tax.[38]

Placing a heavily subsidized rental program into the "sale of tax losses for profit" world stacks the cards in favor of higher cost units. In effect the developer converts into cash the available tax benefits, of which the deduction for depreciation is the most important. The size of this deduction is determined by the amount spent in developing the building. The developer is thus penalized if he attempts to save money during construction. This occurs in a number of ways:

(1) The more a project costs, the greater its tax shelter. A reduction in the cost results in a reduction in the mortgage, which in turn reduces the available tax benefits and lowers the syndication price of the project's equity.

(2) The mortgagor's return is equal to 6 percent of the 11.11 percent of the mortgage amount. The lower the mortgage amount, the lower the return.

(3) The size of the construction fee and other fees paid out during the construction process is based on a percentage of cost. Therefore, the developer is penalized rather than rewarded for efficiency.

Of course, higher costs and higher rents reduce the potential market for a project's units. The effect of this factor is diluted by the subsidy, which results in rents approximately 35 percent below the unsubsidized economic rent of the unit. And just as the market constraints are diluted by the subsidy, the usual HUD constraints are diluted by the nature of the subsidy payment. A $1,000 increase in cost results in an increase in the monthly subsidy per tenant of only a few dollars. The increase in cost need not even result in increased expense to the government if the project can draw higher-income (and therefore higher rent-paying) tenants.

The increased initial costs can also be justified on the basis of improving the economic soundness of the project. The mortgage that is insured is to be amortized over forty years. If economic obsolescence is not to come substantially before physical obsolescence, the building should contain many features that are considered "luxuries" today, but which will be considered "necessities" tomorrow.

The flaws in the scheme are (1) that government costs continually rise, (2) that the number of poor households served by the program continually declines, and (3) that builders can safely produce Section 236 units in markets with high vacancy rates.

Minimized federal presence. The program involves extensive federal regulation. FHA processing, insurance, and supervision of management and rental schedules for a forty-year period is a prerequisite for participation. The government review process for each multifamily project is long and tedious. This results in part from past scandal in the multifamily programs and in part from insulation from the market through the subsidized interest rate. This insulation leads developers to seek the largest possible mortgage rather than the most marketable units. The red tape and regulations add to the cost of Section 236 units so that their "market rent" is above the rent of comparable nonsubsidized units. This means that households with rising incomes and falling subsidies move out of the developments, rather than remaining as the program assumes, because their housing dollars can purchase more in the private market.

Consumer choice. The Section 236 program offers moderate income households a chance to live in new, carpeted, and air-conditioned dwellings in developments with swimming pools for the same price they would have to pay for standard dwellings without these amenities. The subsidy is not available for standard units in other locations built without an agreement with the government.

Minimized opportunity for fraud. The federal commitment to insure and subsidize the project amounts to granting a hunting license in a game preserve. The surprising thing is not the occasional case of corruption, but rather that the case is occasional.

Minimized inequity. Section 236 has the same set of inequities as Section 235. A letter to a congressman from a concerned constituent states one of the political problems of the program.

> As a member of the usually silent majority and an ardent supporter of yours, I believe that I should bring to your attention some things that, from my point of view, should be

corrected. First of all, I am a young man of 25 employed as the personnel supervisor of a growing concern in the area where my wife is also employed. Between us we earn approximately eleven thousand dollars per year and live within our means in a modest three-room apartment in a 40-year-old building. A new (subsidized) housing area . . . is now open for tenants who earn less than six thousand per annum. These apartments are as large or larger than ours, and in beautiful condition and the rent is actually less than I am paying. Is it possible that this situation can be justified? [39]

Where Is the Fault?

The failure of the existing housing programs as judged by the policy criteria used here may be attributable to either managerial or structural faults. Are the deficiencies primarily the result of HUD's inability to run a tight ship or are they the result of the lack of seaworthiness of the present subsidy?

In answering this question, we are fortunate in having Anthony Downs's thorough and well-written recent study, *Federal Housing Subsidies: Their Nature and Effectiveness, and What We Should Do About Them.*[40] Downs, without being oversanguine about the equity and efficiency of existing programs, nevertheless concludes that the current approach is a sound basis for future progress in meeting the nation's housing goal. He states: "It is certainly true that existing housing subsidy programs have many deficiencies and have generated serious problems in some areas. Nevertheless, we believe most of the diffculties do not result from serious structural inadequacies in the major existing programs."[41]

To support this conclusion, Downs lists twenty-nine recommendations for improving the three major housing subsidy programs —public housing, Section 235 and Section 236. Five of his more important recommendations are analyzed below in an effort to discover whether they would improve the programs' effectiveness in terms of our policy criteria. The specific recommendations are quoted, arranged, and analyzed by program.

Public Housing. Here is what Downs concludes:

A more adequate per-unit subsidy in lieu of taxes should be paid to the local governments that serve public housing units. It should be an amount close to what such units would pay if market rents were charged and assessments were made under normal local practices. This subsidy should be financed entirely by the federal government as part of its annual contribution, over and above debt service payments.[42]

As an add-on to revenue sharing, this suggestion cannot be faulted. As a housing program, it would add hundreds of extra dollars to the already high federal subsidy per unit and would further limit the numbers of units produced and households assisted, assuming the same level of federal spending.

Downs further suggests that "most additional . . . public housing units should be created in small-scale projects at scattered locations." [43]

That is exactly what HUD has attempted to do unsuccessfully for over two decades. The reason for failure has been opposition from local citizens who have little to gain from the location of public housing units in their neighborhoods and much to lose. As the Douglas Commission concluded, "The objectors . . . are not bad men and women and should not be treated as such. They are, instead, very human. They worry about their savings, their homes, their neighborhoods and their children. . . ." [44] And as Anthony Downs has pointed out elsewhere,

> two of the characteristics of American suburban life which its residents most appreciate are the relative openness of space around each dwelling unit and the easy informality of movement in its neighborhoods without fear of personal insecurity. . . .
>
> This means that every household is necessarily and rightly concerned with the nature of its neighbors regarding certain aspects of their behavior—particularly their public comportment and the way they maintain and use their property. Therefore, it is both reasonable and proper for each household to want to exclude from its own neighborhood people whose behavior would cause a significant deterioration in its own quality of life. Thus, we are driven to the inescapable conclusion that residential discrimination among households is an inevitable and even desirable characteristic of effective urban living. In fact, as every intelligent observer knows, discrimination of various kinds is an essential ingredient in the living patterns of all people everywhere.[45]

Section 235. On this Downs remarks that

> very low-income households should not be encouraged to undertake homeownership because of the relative hardships imposed upon them in meeting unexpected operating costs,

and the resulting high probability of default. Hence, more formal minimum income requirements should be instituted for Section 235 units.[46]

How low is "very low" in a program aimed at "lower" income households? Is it lower than $4,000? If so, it is meaningless, since these households are already priced out of the market by the economics of the program. If not, how can a program which offers high subsidies only to those who do not need assistance be justified?

Section 236. Finally, here are Downs's conclusions on Section 236:

> HUD should review estimated project costs with far more care and more emphasis upon actual local experience with existing Section 236 projects. This is necessary to avoid cost underestimation—especially of property taxes—and to prevent requests for rent increases arising very soon after a project is occupied. . . .[47]

> More amenities should be allowed (e.g. air conditioning, carpets, swimming pools) so that 236 units remain competitive with non-subsidized units and hold middle-income occupants.[48]

If the first recommendation were adopted, not only would it be impossible to fulfill the recommendation to seek more project amenities, but the entire program would be likely to come to a halt. Section 236's production successes are directly attributable to the powerful leverage resulting from a 1 percent interest rate. With each dollar of net income capable of supporting approximately $27 of debt service, the Section 236 program has found little difficulty in building attractive projects in all areas of the country. Given the large subsidy, it is noteworthy not that the program has had a 90 percent success rate, but rather that some of its projects have failed.

However, leverage is a two-edged sword, and use of realistic expense estimates could topple the entire structure. If one starts with realistic estimates of prospective tenant income and of typical operating expenses, one discovers there is insufficient income to support a mortgage large enough to finance the structural elements of the program, let alone carpets, air conditioning, and swimming pools. With a gross income for a four-person household of $6,000 (which is slightly above the average for the households currently being served) and operating expenses of $1,000, the maximum mortgage allowable for a typical two-bedroom unit is around $6,000. A slow-motion replay is helpful here.

The gross income of $6,000 must first be adjusted by deducting $300 for each child and 5 percent of the remainder, yielding an adjusted income of $5,130. The program assumption that a household will pay 25 percent of its adjusted income for housing yields gross rental income of $1,283. A standard processing adjustment of 5 percent to cover vacancy loss gives a figure of $1,219. A final deduction of $1,000 for all nondebt service expenses leaves only $219 available for debt service. In the nonprofit situation in which a mortgage equal to the full replacement value is possible, the maximum mortgage that could be supported by the $219 available for amortization would be $6,570. In the more typical limited-profit situation, the maximum mortgage would be $5,913. The steps in this process are set forth here:

1. Gross income (husband, wife, two minor children) $6,000
2. Adjustments
   Deduction of $300 per child ($600) 5,400
   95 percent of $5,400 5,130
3. Gross rental income (25 percent of adjusted income) 1,283
4. Effective gross rental income 1,219
5. Operating expense 1,000
6. Net rental income 219
7. Replacement cost 6,570
8. Maximum typical mortgage (90 percent of replacement cost) 5,913

One stroke of realism can kill the goose that laid the golden egg. The recommended administrative improvements merely bring into sharper relief the basic structural faults of the Section 236 program.

A Final Defense

Despite the poor performance of the various federal housing programs and despite the poor prognosis for successful treatment, there is one last defense for the existing programs. It may be claimed that nothing better is at hand. The remainder of this monograph is devoted to presenting alternative programs designed to satisfy the criteria for effective housing programs.

By way of introduction to the subsequent sections, the distinction to be emphasized is that between programs directly aiding production and programs of financial assistance. Each program is designed and evaluated in terms of the respective criteria. Nevertheless, in spite of this conceptual and programmatic division between the two components, they may be considered complementary parts of a single policy to provide a decent home for every household.

In order to prevent inflationary pressures that will be costly not only to the government but also to lower middle-income households, the programs to aid production are made an integral part of the strategy for assistance. The assistance programs are to be used in areas where the supply of adequate housing is sufficient. In other areas the effects of the assistance programs will be supported by the production programs. It may be noted that the primary reason for shifting resources into housing construction is the existence of a housing gap that forces poor people into inadequate housing. As this gap is closed the reason for the production program ceases.[49]

CHAPTER III

ALTERNATIVE
PRODUCTION PROGRAMS

The objective of the three programs proposed here is to produce more housing as long as the need for additional units exists. Their justification is the need for additional dwellings up to the point where a decent unit exists for every family. They are intended to eliminate the shortage of decent housing by enabling private builders to build for markets that would not exist without the programs. Unlike present programs they are not subsidies to bridge the gap between what the builder must receive to produce new dwellings and what the poor can afford to pay.

The main feature of the three programs is their use of the subsidy as a lever to widen the market. In two of them, maximum leverage is obtained by harnessing the subsidy to the income cycle of young, mobile households. The programs retain the basic checks and balances of the marketplace. By dissolving the distinction between subsidized and nonsubsidized developments, they minimize the need for federal regulation and supervision. The government becomes the beneficiary of the market relationship between consumer and producer.

Since the proposed programs are national in character, they are neutral with respect to issues of community development. No attempt is made to engage in social restructuring by altering the locational decisions of target households. These are decisions better made at the state and local level. The proposed subsidies are designed so that they can be supplemented by state and local subsidies that have explicit community development objectives.

New programs in the sales, rental, and elderly fields are set forth below. Each approach will be described and evaluated in terms of the production policy criteria.

Sales Program—Pay As You Grow

In the 1930s FHA transformed the housing industry by introducing a "pay as you go" plan of mortgage finance, featuring low down payments and long-term fully amortized loans. In the 1970s, borrowing from Swedish and Danish experience,[1] HUD could offer a "pay as you grow" plan, featuring an amortization schedule keyed to the household income cycle. Currently, because of level debt service payments, millions of households are priced out of the market due to low current income, although they have a high probability of permanent income more than sufficient to finance a new house. Under the proposed scheme, the household head who today has to wait until his mid-thirties to buy a new house could afford one while still in his twenties.

The key to the scheme is the replacement of the level debt service payment schedule with a rising debt service schedule. This would bring the loan/repayment cycle into closer alignment with the household income of young families. A rising debt service schedule would start with a payment equivalent to that for a below-market-interest-rate mortgage. If the prevailing interest rate were 8 percent, the first year's payment under the new scheme could be the equivalent of the payment required to amortize a mortgage with an interest rate of 5 percent. The payment would increase thereafter, say by 4 percent a year, so that in the later years of the loan the annual payment would be higher under this scheme than under the conventional level-payment method. As Table 2 indicates, on a $25,000 loan amortized over thirty years, the difference in the initial years' interest and principal payment between "pay as you grow" and the conventional method would be approximately $600. If we assume additional housing expenses of approximately $1,000 a year, the annual housing costs under "pay as you grow" would be $2,600 as compared to $3,200. Using a housing expense-to-income ratio of 25 percent, this would give a household with an income of $10,400 access to a market formerly limited to households with incomes of $12,800. The potential market for new units would be thereby increased by approximately 7,000,000 households; and builders would need to attract only one out of thirty-five households in this category to increase production by 200,000 units.

The use of an initial interest rate 3 percentage points below the market is only illustrative. The actual initial interest rate could be adjusted to take into consideration such factors as the supply conditions in local housing markets and the general level of interest rates. The differential could be greater in areas with severe short-

Table 2

COMPARISON OF CONVENTIONAL AND "PAY AS YOU GROW" PAYMENT SCHEDULES
($25,000 8% mortgage, 30 years)

	(1)	(2)	(3)	(4)
Year	Level Payment[a]	Rising by 4% Annually	Difference (1) − (2)	Government Advance Outstanding
1	$2,201	$1,611	$ 590	$ 590
2	2,201	1,675	526	1,116
3	2,201	1,742	459	1,575
4	2,201	1,812	389	1,964
5	2,201	1,884	317	2,281
6	2,201	1,959	242	2,523
7	2,201	2,037	164	2,687
8	2,201	2,118	83	2,770
9	2,201	2,203	− 2	2,768
10	2,201	2,291	− 90	2,678
11	2,201	2,383	− 182	2,496
12	2,201	2,478	− 277	2,219
13	2,201	2,577	− 376	1,843
14	2,201	2,680	− 479	1,364
15	2,201	2,787	− 586	778
16	2,201	2,898	− 697	81

[a] Figures from *Improved Payment Tables for Monthly Mortgage Loans* (Boston: Financial Publishing House, 1967).

ages and smaller (or entirely eliminated) in areas with adequate supplies. Moreover, the program could provide the federal government with a tool for partially insulating the homebuilding industry from exposure to changes in monetary policy, if that is found desirable.

In all likelihood, for families with young heads of households, rising mortgage payments under the plan would be more than matched by rising family income. Future incomes of young families reflect not only general economic trends but specific career promotions. Increasing income means that the majority of these families would be sound risks.[2]

Since lenders would receive a smaller payment during the initial years (which would increase their risk), government advances to lenders might be needed to cover the difference between the level mortgage payment (principal and interest) and the "pay as you grow" payment during these years. These sums, however, would be recovered in later years out of the borrower's higher amortization payments. The payment rate in later years would exceed the uniform payment rate until such time as the government advances were repaid—not taking into account the time value of money.

The program would be limited to young purchasers of new, moderately priced houses who could not afford them if they had to make level payments but who were otherwise good risks. A moderately priced house would be defined as one valued at the lesser figure of (1) the prototype cost (established by the secretary of HUD) for a new house of a similar size in the particular housing market and (2) a unit whose price stands at the lower end of the price scale (25 percent level) for new houses of a similar size in the locality. (This latter requirement would act as an independent check on HUD's cost estimates.) The program would be limited to households that without "pay as you grow" amortization could not afford the cost of owning the moderately priced home without spending more than 25 percent of their gross income for housing expenses. HUD would fix operating expenses by using data for comparable homes in the area.

The program would not require FHA processing and mortgage insurance as a prerequisite for eligibility. Lenders are traditionally prudent and would be likely to require mortgage insurance. With increasing competition from private insurers, the program would not have to rely solely on FHA insurance.

Evaluation. Measured against the policy criteria, the program appears promising.

Performance. Since it would enable builders to serve an otherwise nonexistent market, the program should be effective in increasing production.

Efficiency. Even if every loan went sour immediately after the termination of the advances (when the government subsidy would be at its maximum), the cost would be less than $2,800 per unit—approximately one-third the projected per-unit cost of the Section 235 program. To the extent that the FHA were used, the program might result in income to the government.

General applicability. Since mortgage and eligibility limits would depend on local housing costs, the program would have general applicability.

Effective incentives. By limiting the price of the house, by requiring at least a 5 percent downpayment, by making it clear that the buyer must eventually pay for his purchase, by opening the program to all builders, and by requiring the buyer to satisfy traditional credit standards, the plan would impose market discipline on buyer, builder, and banker.

Consumer choice. The granting of the subsidy commitment to the prospective purchaser rather than to a builder would give the former a wider choice as to the price, type, size, and location of the unit.

Minimized federal presence. The plan would maintain the federal presence but eliminate the need for FHA insurance and long-term supervision. If the buyer and the unit purchase price qualified, the only distinguishing marks of the transaction would be an initial HUD inspection and the unusual mortgage terms.

Minimized opportunity for fraud. Under the Section 235 program, the government is authorizing a select few developers to offer their wares at a substantial discount. In such a case a builder may be willing to pay a high price for a commitment. Under the proposed program, the government would be making a key factor (money) more available for a whole class of buyers. Since the program would be open to all builders and lenders, there would be less reason for individual builders and lenders to curry favor with the federal bureaucracy.

Minimized inequity. By minimizing the subsidy amount, by spreading it among many prospective home buyers, and by providing for repayment of the federal advances, the program would minimize inequity.

Condominiums for the Elderly—Old in New

Based on a priori analysis, "pay as you grow" would work for families with growing incomes. Can an equally workable program be designed to serve a market with stable or decreasing income?

The answer is yes. The market with stable or decreasing income consists of elderly households. There are several economic advantages to serving this market. First, the elderly comprise a substantial segment of the housing problem that our present programs attempt to address. If an appreciable portion of these households could be served by a less costly program, substantial savings would be generated. Second, one of the expected problems in a housing assistance program is the limited availability of appropriate large units for large families. A program that induced older householders to choose new, smaller units would make older and larger units available for younger families.

Nearly two-thirds of elderly couples and persons own homes (debt free, in the vast majority of cases) and many of them face serious housing problems. Rising real estate taxes, rising maintenance costs, and the inability to "do it themselves," when coupled with lower income, make it difficult for the elderly to keep their homes in a good state of repair. This "milking" of their property is to their own as well as to society's disadvantage. In addition, the usual home is designed for larger households at an early stage in the family cycle.

As a result, the elderly often under-occupy shelter that is ill-designed for their use, while younger families (because of low income) are crowded or living in apartments unsuited for rearing children. The condominium program described here would contribute to solving both of these housing problems in a way that would maximize the satisfaction of the households involved and minimize the cost to taxpayers.

The program would be open to all elderly households moving into newly built condominium units and residing there for at least nine months of the year. For purposes of this program, an "elderly" household would be defined as one whose head was fifty-five years of age or over. A condominium arrangement (whether a high-rise, a garden-type or a town-house project) is perfectly suited for elderly occupancy since each household owns its unit and a proportionate share of common space and can make mortgage arrangements to suit its economic situation.

Debt service subsidies in the present Section 235 program work to the disadvantage of the elderly who desire as low a mortgage as possible. The subsidy in the proposed condominium scheme would be tied to the nondebt service components (that is, taxes, insurance, and operating expenses) of housing cost, and it would be paid only when maintenance expenses exceeded 15 percent of household income and limited to the amount in excess of 15 percent of income. Thus, the program would protect elderly owners from rises in housing costs that were not matched by income increases. However, to ensure that owners did not take a free ride on maintenance costs, the subsidy would be further limited to 50 percent of the first $500 of nondebt service costs, 25 percent of the second $500, and 10 percent of any amount over $1,000, up to a level to be set by regulation. The maximum subsidy for a unit with nondebt service expenses of $1,100 would be $385 ($250 [50 percent of $500] + $125 [25 percent of $500] + $10 [10 percent of $100]).

The program would be workable in many areas of the country for households that currently qualify for public housing, and it would be workable in all areas for households that qualify for Section 236 subsidies. The program could (1) eliminate a major

38

cause of concern for elderly households and (2) increase housing production at a relatively low cost. A typical one-bedroom unit costs approximately $16,000 at the present time. The value of the elderly person's existing home is likely to be such that he could net $10,000 on its sale.[3] If the $10,000 were used as a down payment on the new unit, the mortgage would be $6,000. The monthly payment on a $6,000 mortgage (assuming forty-year amortization and a 7½ percent interest rate) would be $39.49 a month. Assuming maintenance costs of $720 a year, the total monthly payment would be $99.49. A household with an annual income of $5,000 would not need a subsidy. A $4,000 annual income would qualify for a $120 subsidy, and a $2,000 income a $305 subsidy (the maximum subsidy being $250 [50 percent of $500] + $55 [25 percent of $220]).

In calculating household income for subsidy purposes, the value of the household's assets (including the equity in the new unit) would be taken into account. This is especially important in a program for the elderly for whom current income is not a sure guide to financial ability.

Evaluation. Measured against the policy criteria, the program, like "pay as you grow," appears promising.

Performance. The combination of ownership without heavy maintenance responsibilities and a government subsidy that reduces rising housing expenses should be an attractive housing package for hundreds of thousands of elderly homeowners.

Efficiency. The program would help elderly households at a fraction of the cost of present programs. It would also make more effective use of resources and the existing housing stock by making available large currently under-occupied houses as a by-product of the production of new units.

General applicability. The program would be generally applicable in all regions. The higher cost of new units in more expensive areas would be likely to be balanced by the higher value of existing homes in these areas.

Effective incentives. The sliding scale of the subsidy payment, plus the fact that many of the households in the condominium would not be subsidized, would serve to brake any tendency toward extravagant maintenance.

Consumer choice. The program would offer the moderate-income elderly households a choice of any new condominium, a choice not confined to only those units built specifically for subsidized owners.

Minimized federal presence. The entire financing, construction and management process could be completely outside the federal domain. Neither the builder-manager of a condominium for the elderly, nor the other occupants, would need to know about the subsidy.

Minimized opportunity for fraud. Since the units would be privately financed and owned, the possibility of the government being "hustled" would be slight.

Minimized inequity. Subsidies would be small and would be directed to an obviously worthy segment of the society. The freeing of larger units for growing families could be regarded as a by-product purchased by the program.

Rental Program—a Carrot Not a Crutch

The rental program, like the other two production programs, would attempt to increase effective demand for new housing. The program would dissolve the present distinction between subsidized and non-subsidized projects. At the financing level, subsidies would be available to new units whether or not they were insured by the federal government. The dollar amount per unit would be substantially smaller than under existing programs, and the percentage of fully subsidized units in any project would also be a fraction of the current total.

The key to the rental program is the establishment of a new market and time frame. The fact that the program would be aimed only at increasing production and not at maintaining long-range financial assistance would enable the relationship between government and producer to be shorter and less involved. The subsidy would be a carrot and not a crutch. What would be provided would be a reward for competence, and the drop in the subsidy amount would be matched by an increase in profit margins, if the producer competently manufactured, marketed, and managed his merchandise.

Under the program, the subsidy would be available only for occupancy of new buildings and only to the initial tenant. The beneficiary of the subsidy would be required to pay at least 20 percent of his income for rent. The subsidy would be the lesser of (1) the difference between the rent and 20 percent of his income and (2) 20 percent of the rent. The unit's rent would have to be equal to or less than the rent of a well-designed and well-managed middle-income unit in the locality.

The program would operate in this way. For each housing market, HUD, with the advice of local housing experts, would set a maximum fair market rental, taking into consideration both local housing costs and the size and type of the dwelling (for example,

$250 for a two-bedroom unit in a garden-type development). The subsidy would be available to all developers of new units under the fixed rents. The developer, when the units were ready for occupancy, would certify to HUD that his rents were at or below the amount set and would receive a commitment for a full subsidy of $50 a month for 20 percent of his units. For a 100-unit project, the total subsidy would be $1,000 a month.

The developer would be free to distribute the $1,000 allocation any way he chose. He could reduce the rents for twenty of the units by $50 each, or for 100 of the units by $10 each, or in any other combination or permutation, as long as (1) no unit subsidy exceeded $50, (2) the subsidy was used for moderate-rent units, and (3) the beneficiary spent more than 20 percent of his income on rent. The developer would choose the tenants and present an income certification to HUD.

The landlord would not have to use the commitment. Under the plan, he would be free to rent without the benefit of the subsidy to anyone and at any rent. In fact, the rent on a unit would be fixed (rent would be adjusted annually on a market-wide basis to take into account changes in operating expenses) only as long as a subsidized tenant lived in it. If the tenant graduated out of the subsidy or moved out of the apartment, the subsidy would be forever lost and the landlord would have complete freedom to set the new rent for that unit.

Evaluation. Measured against the policy criteria, the program, like the two outlined above, seems to promise more new housing at lower cost to government than is provided under current programs.

Performance. Assuming a 20 percent rent/income ratio, the $600 a year subsidy would greatly expand the market for new housing. If we posit a $250 per month rental, the market would be extended to households with incomes over $12,000 whereas otherwise it is limited to households with incomes over $15,000. In 1969 there were over 7 million households whose incomes fell between $12,000 and $15,000.

Efficiency. Considering normal growth and tenant turnover, the likely per-unit subsidy cost over the life of the project would be between $1,000 and $2,000. This amount is somewhere between one-tenth and one-fortieth of the expected run-out cost of the Section 236 program. By limiting the subsidy to units (1) for which the initial occupant pays more than 20 percent of income and (2) which have moderate rentals, the subsidy would be aimed at renters who would otherwise be priced out of the market.

General applicability. By requiring that maximum rentals be related to local conditions, which in turn would determine the subsidy amounts received by families in the area, the general applicability of the program would be ensured.

Effective incentives. By limiting the subsidy, the market framework would be retained. The developer would be forced by conditions of supply and demand to be responsive to consumer desires and local market conditions and to operate as efficiently as possible.

Consumer choice. The program would enable the subsidized household to choose among a wide variety of new buildings and locations. Projects could tailor the subsidy amount to more or fewer units within the project which, in turn, would provide a wider variety of projects and choices.

Minimized federal presence. The program would get the government out of the retail business of reviewing individual housing project applications. At the same time, it would reduce the length of the government's involvement in a project from the present forty years to an estimated five.

Minimized opportunity for fraud. Although opportunities for chiseling are always present, the extension of the program to the maximum number of projects, with a limit on the proportion of units covered in any one, would reduce the possibility of favoritism in the allocation of the subsidy.

Minimized inequity. A short-run widespread subsidy would minimize unfairness. The general effect would be to increase the housing costs of middle-income families participating in the program by upgrading the quality of their housing and to decrease the housing costs of lower-income families by increasing the stock of housing.

CHAPTER IV

ALTERNATIVE
ASSISTANCE PROGRAMS

The objective of the assistance program proposed below is to enable every household to pay for decent housing. Its justification is the assumption that the community has an obligation for the general welfare of all its citizens. The program differs from existing housing assistance in that it has no production component. It is intended to provide poor households with the means to pay for decent existing units, not to directly produce new units. Indeed, it is assumed that the source of units for the program would be the existing stock of 60 million standard units, and that substandard housing would be destroyed or upgraded as the occupants moved out. The production programs suggested in Chapter III can be expected to increase the stock of housing directly whereas the assistance program discussed here would work to that end indirectly.

The primary target of the program is the "poor." The "poor" could be defined as either those households with incomes below the Social Security Administration's poverty thresholds or those with incomes below 50 percent of the median income level in the local housing market area. Either definition would be workable for a housing assistance program. Use of the SSA's poverty threshold might be preferable, because the proliferation of eligibility requirements is one factor that complicates the development of a coherent national strategy against poverty.

The proposed assistance program is meant to encompass all eligible households, not just the small percentage now benefited by existing federal housing programs. Coverage could be extended to this full constituency in stages to enable the phasing out of existing programs and to soften the initial impact on the federal budget.

The program would provide poor households with the widest possible choice of housing. Subsidies are designed to reward the family that chooses to upgrade its housing substantially. However, if a family wishes to limit its expenditure for housing and, as a result, chooses substandard quarters, its decision would be accepted. The government would have fulfilled its obligation by providing the family with the means to pay for decent housing. For the government to go further and force families into rigid expenditure patterns would be a cure more unpleasant than the illness.

Willingness to grant the poor a choice in housing (and not to require that assisted households live in standard units) is entirely consistent with a local government policy of eliminating substandard units through code enforcement and other means. Indeed, a housing assistance program that provided poor households (many of which are currently living in substandard units) with the means to pay for upgraded units meeting code requirements would remove one of the main stumbling blocks to local upgrading efforts. Although the program is not focused on housing conservation, the availability of housing dollars for the poor would almost certainly result in improving the nation's housing stock by increasing the demand for well-maintained, older properties even in low-income areas.

An Assistance Program: Private Housing

The subsidy a household would receive under the proposed program would depend on the household's size, income, and the quality of the unit it chose as a residence. In this respect the plan differs from current arrangements. First, under existing programs, there is no relationship between family size and income on the one hand and size of subsidy on the other. A single person living in a new public housing unit may be receiving a far larger benefit than a family of ten in an old unit. Under the proposed alternative, the larger the family with a given income the larger the subsidy. Second, under existing programs, a family with an income higher than that of another family of equal size may be receiving a much greater subsidy. An $8,000 family in a $24,000 Section 235 home receives a larger subsidy than a $4,000 family in a $12,000 home. Under the proposal, the poorer family would receive the larger subsidy. Third, under existing programs, the rent a household pays is often unrelated to the quality of the unit. The household living in a new suburban public housing unit will often pay the same rent as the household living in an old unit in an inner city area. Under the proposal, the rent a household would pay for a unit would vary directly with the quality of the unit. Finally, under existing programs, the required rent/income ratio is high and rigid whereas, under the proposal, a household would have a wide choice as to the amount it allocates for housing.

All of this would be accomplished by replacing the one-dimensional rental formula used in present programs (which narrows the scope of consumer decision making) with a matrix which would widen the variety of housing options. Table 3 shows a subsidy schedule based on the concept.

The subsidy a household would receive would be determined by household size (the vertical column) and the rent/income ratio (the horizontal row). A family unwilling to spend 15 percent of its income on rent would receive no subsidy. The program would create a strong incentive for the household to spend more than 15 percent by providing a subsidy equal to approximately two-thirds of the rental over the 15 percent level until a rent/income ratio of 20 percent was reached. Between the 20 and 25 percent rent/income ratio levels, the federal government would pay half the additional rental and, between 25 and 31 percent, the federal share would drop to one-third. The government would not share in any increase in cost when the rent rose above 31 percent.

The table sets $700 as the proper amount of annual subsidy for a four-person household spending 25 percent of its income on rent. This is a pragmatic choice, and it must be emphasized that there are two conflicting objectives that this choice has to satisfy. It must be high enough to give poor households a choice from among decent housing units, and it must be low enough so that the expansion of the program to the entire universe of eligible households would be acceptable to taxpayers not directly benefiting from the program. Table 4 indicates how the subsidy would combine with the tenant's payment at different rent and income levels (assuming a four-person household).

Will the Program Work? Two questions concerning the program arise. First, is it administratively workable? Could it be administered without the aid of a large cadre of bureaucrats? Second, are the numbers realistic—that is, would they permit poor households a real choice?

Program administration. The applicant for housing assistance would get in touch with the local administering agency—in most areas, the local housing authority (LHA)—where he would certify his income and his household size. Income would include gross income as defined for income tax purposes, plus transfer payments

Table 3

SUBSIDY SCHEDULE FOR THE PROPOSED ASSISTANCE PROGRAM

(in dollars)

Annual Subsidy at Various Rent/Income Ratios

Persons in Household	Over 30%	30%	29%	28%	27%	26%	25%	24%	23%	22%	21%	20%	19%	18%	17%	16%	15%	Under 15%
1	$460	450	440	430	420	410	400	380	360	340	320	300	260	220	180	140	100	0
2	475	563	550	538	525	513	500	475	450	425	400	375	325	275	225	175	125	0
3	690	675	660	645	630	615	600	570	540	510	480	450	390	330	270	210	150	0
4	800	788	770	753	735	718	700	665	630	595	560	525	455	385	315	245	175	0
5	920	900	880	860	840	820	800	760	720	680	640	600	520	440	360	280	200	0
6	1,035	1,013	990	968	945	923	900	855	810	765	720	675	585	495	405	315	225	0
7	1,150	1,125	1,100	1,075	1,050	1,025	1,000	950	900	850	800	750	650	550	450	350	250	0

Table 4

TENANT AND GOVERNMENT CONTRIBUTION AT VARIOUS RENT AND INCOME LEVELS UNDER PROPOSED PROGRAM
(Four-person household)

	Annual Income				
	$2,000	$2,500	$3,000	$3,500	$4,000
Rent	$ 475	$ 550	$ 625	$ 700	$ 775
15% tenant contribution	300	375	450	525	600
Government subsidy	175	175	175	175	175
Rent	925	1,025	1,125	1,225	1,325
20% tenant contribution	400	500	600	700	800
Government subsidy	525	525	525	525	525
Rent	1,200	1,325	1,450	1,575	1,700
25% tenant contribution	500	625	750	875	1,000
Government subsidy	700	700	700	700	700
Rent	1,388	1,538	1,688	1,838	1,988
30% tenant contribution	600	750	900	1,050	1,200
Government subsidy	788	788	788	788	788

(for example, public assistance or unemployment compensation) and the value of in-kind benefits (for example, food stamps). A deduction of 10 percent would be allowed from total earned income. As a check on the accuracy of the certification, a copy of the previous year's tax return would be filed. (Clearly this proposal would be aided by reform in the administration of other federal assistance programs. For example, (1) a social security number could be required of all applicants and (2) a central information assistance record could be kept to permit quick verification of the accuracy of reporting with regard to public welfare programs. Even without these reforms, administrative costs should be relatively low.)

The applicant, if eligible, would be supplied with a rent table appropriate to his income and household size (see Table 5). The table would set forth the respective tenant and federal government contributions for different monthly rent levels at $1 intervals. The tenant would then shop for housing. When he returned with an executed lease (or certified his rent and address), the federal subsidy would be calculated and the monthly check would be sent him at that address. He would be required to report any rent decrease of more than 10 percent and to certify his income every year.

Table 5

PROPOSED RENT TABLE: FOUR-PERSON HOUSEHOLD,
$4,000 INCOME

Monthly Rent	Tenant Contribution	Government Subsidy
$110	$66	$44
111	67	44
112	67	45
113	68	45
114	68	46
115	69	46
116	69	47
117	70	47
118	70	48
119	71	48
120	71	49

As an alternative approach, the LHA could keep an inventory of units that it would lease (as under the present Section 23 leasing program) and eligible households could shop among those units. The main difference between this and the first approach is that the tenants would have no direct legal relationship with the landlord. Rather they would be subtenants of the authority. Although this alternative would limit tenant choice, it has a number of advantages. A local housing authority has greater bargaining power in the market than the average single tenant. In addition, the low risk of dealing with a government agency and the certainty that rent checks would be delivered regularly should be reflected in lower rents, at least for marginal tenants. It must be realized, however, that this variation would increase the government presence.

Are the numbers realistic? The best way to test the realism of the numbers is to ask whether the subsidy schedule would enable the poor to purchase decent housing with relatively modest proportions of their modest incomes.

Rent and income figures based on 1970 Bureau of Census data are presented above in Table 1. Table 6 reproduces these data and adds data on the subsidies poor households would require annually (column 4) and monthly (column 5) in these cities in order to enable them to rent their current adequate housing (full plumbing facilities). Column 6 shows the rent/income ratio, or required tenant effort, at the various subsidy figures. Column 7 gives the percentage

Table 6

APPLICABILITY OF PROPOSED ASSISTANCE PROGRAM

	(1) Median Housing Expense of Poor Families[a]	(2) Median Family Income of Working Poor	(3) Rent/Income Ratio	(4)(5) Subsidy Required to Rent Adequate Housing		(6) Rent/Income Ratio	(7) Adequate Private Units as % of Total Units
				Annual	Monthly		
1 New York—all	$90	$3,100	35%	$455	$38	19%	97%
2 Manhattan	89	2,900	37	525	44	20	—
3 Brooklyn	83	3,200	31	385	32	18	—
4 Bronx	90	3,200	34	455	38	19	—
5 Queens	131	2,200	71	800	67	35	—
6 Los Angeles	90	3,200	34	455	38	19	98
7 Chicago	115	2,000	69	788	66	30	96
8 Philadelphia	74	2,600	34	385	32	18	98
9 Detroit	88	1,600	66	665	55	24	97
10 San Francisco	120	2,100	69	800	67	31	93
11 Washington, D. C.	115	3,800	36	560	47	21	98
12 Boston	109	2,000	65	753	63	28	94
13 Pittsburgh	65	3,100	25	245	20	16	93
14 St. Louis	74	2,200	40	455	38	19	93
15 Baltimore, Md.	94	2,400	47	595	50	22	98
16 Cleveland	87	2,300	45	560	47	21	97
17 Houston	80	3,000	32	385	32	18	98

Table 6 (continued)

APPLICABILITY OF PROPOSED ASSISTANCE PROGRAM

		(1) Median Housing Expense of Poor Families[a]	(2) Median Family Income of Working Poor	(3) Rent/Income Ratio	(4) & (5) Subsidy Required to Rent Adequate Housing		(6) Rent/Income Ratio	(7) Adequate Private Units as % of Total Units
					Annual	Monthly		
18	Newark	$114	$2,100	65%	$770	$64	29%	94%
19	Dallas	89	2,800	38	525	44	20	98
20	Minneapolis	110	3,900	34	525	44	20	94
21	St. Paul	92	2,500	44	560	47	21	—
22	Milwaukee	88	2,800	38	525	44	20	96
23	Atlanta	75	2,500	36	385	32	18	98
24	Cincinnati	78	2,400	39	455	38	19	95
25	Buffalo	71	3,100	27	315	26	17	97
26	San Diego	87	2,900	36	455	38	19	98
27	Miami, Fla.	106	2,600	49	665	55	24	95
28	Kansas City, Mo.	76	2,600	35	455	38	19	96
29	Denver	81	3,100	31	385	32	18	96
30	Indianapolis	80	3,000	32	385	32	18	96
31	New Orleans	74	2,900	31	385	32	18	96
32	Oakland, Calif.	94	2,600	43	595	50	22	94
33	Tampa, Fla.	62	3,200	23	245	20	16	96
34	Portland, Oreg.	76	1,700	54	560	47	21	95

35	Phoenix, Ariz.	66	3,500	23	245	20	16	98
36	Columbus, Ohio	76	2,600	35	455	35	19	98
37	San Antonio, Tex.	40	3,600	13	—	—	—	94
38	Dayton, Ohio	69	2,700	31	315	26	17	96
39	Rochester, N. Y.	98	3,500	34	455	38	19	96
40	Louisville, Ky.	63	2,500	30	315	26	17	96
41	Memphis, Tenn.	59	3,100	23	245	20	16	97
42	Fort Worth, Tex.	63	3,200	24	245	20	16	98
43	Birmingham, Ala.	42	2,800	18	—	—	—	97
44	Toledo, Ohio	76	1,900	48	525	44	20	98
45	Akron, Ohio	84	1,900	53	595	50	22	97
46	Norfolk, Va.	71	3,200	27	315	26	17	97
47	Oklahoma City, Okla.	63	3,300	23	245	20	16	97
48	Jersey City, N. J.	92	2,500	44	595	50	22	94
49	Providence, R. I.	72	3,100	28	315	26	17	97
50	Omaha, Nebr.	79	2,200	43	455	38	19	96
51	Youngstown, Ohio	66	2,400	33	385	32	18	97
52	Tulsa, Okla.	63	2,900	26	315	26	17	98
53	Charlotte, N.C.	70	3,000	28	315	26	17	99
54	Wichita, Kans.	66	4,100	19	175	15	15	98
55	Bridgeport, Conn.	117	4,000	35	560	47	21	95
	Summary	83	2,900	34	455	38	19	—

a Mortgage payment or rent plus utilities.

Sources: Columns 1-3, Table 1 above; column 7, U.S. Department of Commerce, *1970 Census of Population and Housing, United States Summary, Final Report*, Table 17 (Washington, D. C.: Government Printing Office, October 1971); for a more detailed explanation of the calculations in columns 4, 5, and 6 see the Appendix.

of units in each city that meet adequacy standards. Since the lowest percentage of adequate units is 93 percent, it is fairly certain that the median rents would purchase adequate accommodations.

In approximately two-thirds of the cities listed, proposed subsidy schedules would enable the poor to rent adequate housing by spending 20 percent or less of their income. Even in the most difficult cities, the program would reduce the ratio to tolerable levels. For example, in Queens, which has the highest median rent and a low median income level ($700 below the average), the ratio would be halved. In other high-rent, low-income areas, the ratio would be reduced to under 30 percent.

These results could be accomplished at a low per-unit cost to the federal government. The average subsidy would be approximately $455 a year, a fraction of the per-unit cost of today's public housing unit. Table 7 compares the federal subsidies (debt service and operating) required for existing public housing units with estimated subsidy levels for existing private housing in twenty-five cities under the proposed plan.

The program described is primarily a rental program. Of the 8 million poor households approximately 4.8 million are renters. Since approximately 45 percent of the poor households are individuals without families, the 4.8 million households would be composed of approximately 2.6 million families (averaging slightly under four persons) and 2.2 million individuals. If the proposed assistance were extended to all of these households, the total annual subsidy would be about $1.7 billion (assuming a subsidy level of $500 per family and $320 per individual).

The program would not be suitable for homeowners. Although the rent figure is conceptually no different than the imputed value of the residence to the owner, there is a world of difference administratively. To extend the program to homeowners would require a huge corps of valuators and, as the numbers grew, the likelihood of uniform valuations would decrease while the opportunities for corruption increased.

A simpler alternative for homeowners would be an assistance program that pegged the subsidy to an independently determined cost factor such as the real property tax. Local property taxes have escalated rapidly and have put a great deal of financial pressure on low-income elderly homeowners. Since in the majority of cases these homes are debt-free, a small assistance payment would not only permit the elderly poor to live in familiar surroundings with dignity but would also prevent the deterioration of the housing stock.

Table 7

COMPARISON OF SUBSIDIES UNDER PUBLIC HOUSING AND ALTERNATIVE ASSISTANCE PLAN

		Public Housing Subsidy			Ratio: Alterna-tive/ Public Housing
		Debt Service[a]	Oper-ating Deficit[b]	Total[c]	Alter-native Sub-sidy[d]	
1	New York	$704	$419	$1,123	$455	.41
2	Los Angeles, Calif.	335	201	536	455	.85
3	Philadelphia, Penn.	497	900	1,397	385	.28
4	Detroit, Mich.	488	435	923	665	.72
5	San Francisco, Calif.	588	613	1,201	800	.67
6	Washington, D. C.	643	2,022	2,665	560	.21
7	St. Louis, Mo.	606	283	889	455	.51
8	Baltimore, Maryland	502	803	1,305	595	.46
9	Houston, Texas	144	18	162	385	2.38
10	Minneapolis, Minn.	707	282	989	525	.53
11	Miami, Fla.	397	245	642	665	1.04
12	Indianapolis, Ind.	1,008	144	1,152	385	.33
13	New Orleans, La.	384	0	384	385	1.00
14	Oakland, Calif.	644	211	855	595	.70
15	Portland, Oreg.	445	317	762	560	.73
16	Phoenix, Ariz.	412	339	751	245	.33
17	Columbus, Ohio	532	163	695	455	.65
18	San Antonio	570	219	789	—	.00
19	Dayton, Ohio	291	117	408	315	.77
20	Birmingham, Ala.	512	167	679	—	.00
21	Akron, Ohio	363	141	504	595	1.18
22	Norfolk, Va.	472	48	520	315	.61
23	Omaha, Neb.	272	195	467	455	.97
24	Youngstown, Ohio	437	172	609	385	.63
25	Charlotte, N. C.	650	12	662	315	.48

[a] From HUD, Office of Financial Systems and Services; based on fiscal 1971 data.
[b] From HUD, Financial Management Division of the Office of Housing Program; based on LHA projected deficits for fiscal 1973.
[c] Does not include federal or local tax expenditure.
[d] Based on Table 6.

The mean value of the home of a poor household in 1969 was approximately $12,000.[1] Census data indicate that single family homes were taxed at an average effective rate of 1.8 percent of true market value. This would result in a tax of $216 per year, an amount that is close to 11 percent of the income of a $2,000 household. Property tax relief along the lines of a number of proposals under consideration in the 93rd Congress could offer housing assistance to homeowners at a low cost to the government. If the federal government refunded all taxes paid in excess of 6 percent of income of poor households, the $2,000 household would receive a rebate of $96 a year—which might be the extra dollars needed to permit proper maintenance and repairs.

As a rule, assistance to homeowners should be lower on a per-unit basis than assistance to renters. For given equal incomes the homeowner is usually in better condition financially than the renter because of the equity value of his home. This suggests that a fair assistance system would take both household assets and income into account. This could be accomplished by adding to income a percentage of assets (for example 5 percent of all assets in excess of $2,000).

Looking abroad, it may be noted that Sweden provides housing allowances to homeowners as well as renters, while England, Denmark and Germany limit allowances to renters.

Evaluation. The program's probable effectiveness is summarized below.

Performance. As the next section of this monograph will indicate, the proposed alternative permits an expansion in the number of households assisted without increasing total federal subsidies in the housing field.

Efficiency. The per-unit costs of the program would be a fraction of per-unit public housing costs. Since the program defines income to include in-kind welfare payments, any additional costs to the government resulting from increased payment levels in other programs would be reflected in lower housing assistance costs.

General applicability. As Table 6 illustrates, the program would be applicable in all areas of the country. The subsidy amount smoothes out geographical differences in housing costs. Other things being equal, a household in a high housing cost area has a higher rent/income ratio and therefore would receive a higher subsidy than a household in a low-cost area. Also, the subsidy schedule could be easily adjusted if the relationship between incomes and rents should change. Changes in this relationship would be reflected in per-unit subsidy levels which, in turn, would be reflected in the rent/income ratios. If rent/income ratios rose, it would indicate that rents were rising faster than income. If it were decided to redress the imbalance, the administrator would need to change only one number in the subsidy table, and the computers would do the rest.

Effective incentives. The proposed program would avoid the dilemma produced by existing assistance programs that are based on bridging a gap between income and housing costs.[2] Under these programs, the household receives the difference between the federally determined cost of housing in the locality and a fixed percentage of its income. The federally determined rent represents an average and therefore, by definition, is above the rent for a substantial number of units of presumably identical size and quality. The very setting of the number, which in any large-scale program is a matter of public information, tends to turn the average into a floor. If the money is earmarked for housing, there is no reason for a household to object if its rent rises to the federally determined rent since the government is footing the entire bill for the increase. The only way to create countervailing pressure from the demand side is to allow the household to pocket the money, but this defeats the stated purpose of the housing subsidy. The proposed assistance program would, however, earmark the allowance without creating a rent floor.

Consumer choice. The consumer would be sovereign in the proposed program. He would determine what housing was properly priced and of the desired quality, and could choose among all the housing stock in his range.

Minimized federal presence. Under the proposed arrangement, the federal government would not be interfering with the market process.

Minimized opportunity for fraud. The proposal entails a series of roadblocks designed to stop possible collusion between landlord and tenant. In order to collude, a tenant would have to tell the landlord his income and that he was receiving assistance (payments would be in cash), so that the subsidy could be computed. The less-than-friendly and often hostile relationship between tenants and landlords would preclude many deals. Moreover, the reward for fraud would be small since any rent increase would have to be split three ways. Assuming the rent was over 20 percent of tenant income, the government would pay, at most, only half of any increase and that half would then have to be shared by the partners. It is unlikely that the amounts to be gained from such fraud would be worth the effort and the risk of criminal sanctions.

Minimized inequity. The major unfairness in subsidy programs results from the setting of rigid eligibility cutoffs. If the income limit for a four-person household is $4,000, the family whose income is $3,999 receives full benefit and the family whose income is $4,001 receives none. This not only creates serious work disincentives for households whose incomes are just below the limit but also enables a household with a lower income to obtain better housing than one with a higher income.

The solution to the problem is a gradual reduction of the subsidy as income levels rise, rather than a single cutoff point. But this solution has its cost. If the subsidy is extended to households on the other side of the income eligibility line, it will be both more equitable and more costly. One version of the proposed housing assistance program would include households with incomes up to about 150 percent of the SSA-defined poverty threshold—currently, about $6,000 for a four-person household. The subsidy could be reduced 10 percent for each additional $200 in income above the $4,000 level.

This extension of the subsidy would more than double the number of persons covered by the program (from an estimated 27 million to about 60 million). Since the average subsidy per household would be approximately half the basic subsidy, the total annual cost of the program would rise by about $1.7 billion to $2.6 billion. A less costly alternative would be to begin reducing the subsidy at a lower figure. Thus, if the full subsidy were available only to households with incomes up to about $3,350 (rather than $4,000), the cutoff point would become $5,000 rather than $6,000, substantially reducing the program's coverage and cost.

Public Housing under the Assistance Program

Is an assistance system compatible with public housing? Can public housing survive if its tenants are able to retain their subsidy if they move elsewhere? The answers to both questions are yes. In fact, the adoption of an assistance program may be the only way to prevent the impending bankruptcy of the public housing program.

An Overview of the Public Housing Crisis. There are three basic interest groups involved in the present public housing problem:

The federal government (that is, the taxpaying public), which pays the full debt service on public housing projects and is now, to the dismay of the Office of Management and Budget, being asked to pick up the tab for ever-increasing operating expense deficits.

Local housing authorities, which find themselves—as a result of federal law and regulation, less than superb management practices, and the widening of the housing options available to low-income households—able to attract only the poorest of the poor as new tenants. Thus, their deficits are rising, and they look to Washington for additional assistance.

Tenants, who look to public housing as the only decent housing they can afford but who find the units deteriorating, often with the active assistance of their neighbors.

The building of new public housing units is not only a poor way to meet the housing needs of the poor, but also creates a vicious cycle with regard to the existing stock of public housing. As data in the Kaiser Commission Report of 1968 indicated, new one-bedroom public housing units in Detroit (a city with relatively low construction costs) would require a minimum rental of $75 per month just to *cover operating expenses.*[3] Assuming that tenants of these units pay rentals equal to 25 percent of income, a minimum income of $3,600 would therefore be necessary. Unfortunately, the income of the households occupying these small units was substantially under $3,600. This example illustrates how the building of new units drains funds from the system and forces the LHA to milk older units by skimping on their maintenance and modernization. The older units, which were once economic bargains, now become attractive only to households with the least choice. By a Gresham's law of public housing, these "bad" tenants drive out the "good" tenants and put public housing in disrepute. In order to change its image, the LHA decides to build new units, and thereby drives itself deeper into trouble.

The Road to Solvency. New public housing units are similar to the Edsel automobile. Not only are they a failure in and of themselves, but they threaten otherwise profitable operations of the company. Instead of building new Edsels like Pruitt-Igoe of St. Louis, the federal government should (1) stop the production of new public housing units, (2) encourage LHAs to dispose of their new projects, and (3) encourage LHAs to compete vigorously for tenants in older units.

Extending the housing assistance program to public housing would permit all of these basic tasks to be done and, in addition, would permit LHAs to serve a larger segment of the low-income market.

The Proposal. The basic features of the program proposed here are as follows: (1) the amount a tenant pays in rent and the amount the government contributes in subsidy would depend on the unit's market rent and the tenant's income; (2) tenants would be given a wide choice with regard to housing location and rent/income ratio;

(3) local housing authorities would be treated to the maximum extent possible as private landlords. At first glance, these features seem inimical to present public housing. Closer examination suggests, however, that the assistance plan would be compatible with public housing and conducive to improved LHA operations. Most important, it would provide better housing opportunities for more low-income families.

Under the present public housing system, both the authorities and their tenants are prisoners of the subsidy. Under the new system, even if a tenant should break his tie with a project, he would continue to be eligible for the subsidy. In like manner, LHAs (state law permitting) would not be limited to serving the very poor. Just as important, LHAs will not be tied to debt service. Although the latter encourages construction, it makes long-term maintenance impossible in the face of rising operating costs and declining revenues. The point of the assistance programs suggested here is that they are not designed to encourage construction but to permit proper allocation of a housing stock already built up by the production programs outlined in Chapter III.

The first step in changing over from the old to the new program would be for local housing authorities to set unit rents to cover full debt service and operating costs. Recently, in a study covering 700,000 public housing units with fiscal years ending in 1969, David Yentis of HUD found that the average economic rent required for the units was $97.93 per month, or $1,175.16 per year.[4]

The second step would be to determine the rent to be paid by the tenant on the basis of income, family size and the rental value of the unit. Table 8 illustrates the proposed scheme. Five different situations are presented for four different income levels. Situation 1 is an older modest unit with a rent of a little over $60 per month and a present subsidy or annual contribution contract (ACC) which covers the debt service subsidy of $385 a year. At all four income levels, the proposed assistance would produce both savings for the federal government (or greater surpluses for the LHA) and low rent/income ratios for tenants. In Situation 2, the rent is raised on the unit (presumably to upgrade housing services). In this situation, the government subsidy would be higher than the ACC by $15 a month ($175 a year) for the $2,000 household and $3 a month ($35 a year) for the $3,000 household, and lower in the other two cases. In all four cases, the rent/income ratio would be low (between 17 and 21 percent). In Situation 3, the average situation in 1969, the added government cost would be $11 a month ($132 a year) at the lowest income level, and $.25 a month (about $3 a year) at $3,000.

Table 8

PUBLIC HOUSING UNDER A NEW SUBSIDY ROOF

	Annual Income for a Four-Person Household			
	$2,000	$3,000	$3,500	$4,000
1. Economic rent–$745				
Present subsidy–385				
Tenant contribution[a]	$360(18%)	$480(16%)	$535(15%)	$745(15%)
Government subsidy	385	265	210	—
Savings (added cost)	—	120	175	385
2. Economic rent–$980				
Present subsidy–385				
Tenant contribution[a]	420(21%)	560(18%)	645(18%)	675(17%)
Government subsidy	560	420	335	305
Savings (added cost)	(175)	(35)	50	80
3. Economic rent–$1,200				
Present subsidy–568				
Tenant contribution[a]	500(25%)	635(21%)	692(20%)	755(19%)
Government subsidy	700	565	508	445
Savings (added cost)	(132)	(3)	60	123
4. Economic rent–$1,500				
Present subsidy–750				
Tenant contribution[a]	700(35%)	781(26%)	842(24%)	893(22%)
Government subsidy	800	718	665	607
Savings (added cost)	(50)	32	85	143
5. Economic rent–$1,800				
Present subsidy–900				
Tenant contribution[a]	900(45%)	900(30%)	1,037(30%)	1,090(27%)
Government subsidy	900	900	788	730
Savings (added cost)	—	—	112	170

[a] Given in dollars and rent/income ratios.

At higher incomes, it would be less expensive. The $2,000 household would reach a 25 percent rent/income ratio, and the others would be at or below 21 percent. In Situation 4, a $125 per month apartment, many of the very lowest income households would be effectively priced out of the market. The other three income levels would have rent/income ratios in the 22-26 percent range and government subsidies would be less than the present debt service obligation. In Situation 5, no additional funds could be paid since the ACC already would exceed the subsidy table maximum. Thus, all four income levels would be required to pay a high proportion of their incomes—at least 30 percent for incomes of $3,500 or less—in order to live in this fairly expensive unit.

Given a framework of this kind, LHAs would find that their most profitable course would be to maintain and refurbish their older units. The savings listed in the table would be, in effect, surplus for the LHA. In Situations 2 and 3, the added costs would be covered because assistance payments to tenants would permit tenants to rent the now more expensive units. The LHAs should be more than able to meet market competition, even when the tenant is given a choice, since they are nonprofit and receive a substantial property tax abatement. The fact that the tenants would no longer be captive of the subsidy system, however, would impose a greater discipline on LHAs than could be imposed by reams of circulars and squadrons of auditors and inspectors. If it turned out that LHAs or, more likely, particular projects could not make it (or, to put it another way, if low-income tenants should find better housing opportunities elsewhere), HUD should not intervene to bail out the projects. Rather, it should advise LHAs to dispose of unprofitable operations.

Under the proposal, public housing's problems (at least those related to structural flaws in the program rather than to poor management) would generally be reduced to those involved in new and expensive high-subsidy projects—since, in these cases, tenants would not qualify for additional subsidies. However, this is not a homogeneous category. It includes projects for the elderly, family projects in good areas, and family projects in bad areas. By and large, the projects for the elderly provide excellent accommodations for elderly households, and enough elderly persons may be able to expend 30 percent or more of their incomes to make these units profitable. The standard budget of the Bureau of Labor Statistics allocates 35 percent of an elderly couple's budget to housing (including shelter, household operations, and home furniture) as compared to 21 percent for a poor, non-elderly family. To the extent that elderly persons are forced to move, HUD should have little difficulty in finding older private units to accommodate them.

With respect to the family projects, it is unlikely that many of their tenants would be able to spend over 30 percent of their incomes on housing. However, if the project is located in or near a good area (which is the case for the infamous Cabrini-Green complex in Chicago), a market for the *structure* would be likely to exist at a price covering the public indebtedness. Upon sale of the structure the outstanding bonds could be retired. As an incentive, HUD could permit the LHA to turn any profits over to the *municipality*. Even without this feature, the prospect of the property's return to the city's tax fold would provide a strong local inducement for selling the unit. As for the expensive projects in bad areas, these structures would also be marketable, although at prices substantially less than development cost. The availability of a housing assistance program would increase demand for standard units and provide customers for the "privatized" units.

Given a new framework of the kind proposed here, LHAs would discover that the way to a profitable future would be to dispose of more expensive units or to attract higher income tenants. In the absence of an assistance plan, either approach would be highly unattractive. However, under the plan, the LHA would not have to choose between economic solvency and social commitment, because the former tenant of the unit would be given assistance to obtain another unit. Given the current state of public housing, this might be an attractive possibility.

CHAPTER V

CONCLUSION

Without diminishing the importance of Murphy's law (if something can go wrong, it will), the proposed programs, though far from perfect, should achieve better results than the existing programs. Nevertheless, the question that remains is whether the new programs can be put into effect without blowing the lid off the federal budget.[1]

Hypothetical Budgets

In order to examine this question, it is useful to compare an annual budget based on existing programs with two budgets based on the proposed strategy, one for a "minimum" level of assistance and one for a "maximum" level.[2] All three assume an annual level of 480,000 starts—a slight rise from the estimated 464,000 reservations for new units requested in the administration's fiscal 1973 budget.[3]

Old Programs in an Old Budget. A typical post-1968 HUD housing budget is composed of one part production for poor families (public housing and rent supplements) and three parts production for "lower" income families (Sections 235 and 236).[4] Based on 480,000 starts, this mix would produce 120,000 public housing and rent supplement units and 360,000 interest subsidy units. The first hypothetical budget in Table 9 illustrates the cost of this addition to the subsidized housing stock. The unit costs used for the interest subsidy programs are $900 (see Chapter II) and those for the production-for-the-poor programs have been rounded off to $2,000 a year. As for the public housing operating subsidy, HUD's estimate for fiscal 1974 is $280 million,[5] and the congressional appropriations

Table 9

ESTIMATED COSTS OF ALTERNATIVE HOUSING BUDGETS [a]

	No. of Units Produced	No. of Additional Households Assisted	1st Year Cost/Unit	1st Year Cost (millions)	Total Cost[b] (millions)	Per Unit Total
1. OLD PROGRAMS						
a. Public housing and rent supplement	120,000	120,000	$2,000	$240	$ 9,600	80,000
b. Section 235	180,000	—	900	162	1,620	9,000
Section 236	180,000	—	900	162	4,500	25,000
c. Public housing operating subsidy	—	—	—	300	12,000	—
	480,000	120,000		$864	$27,720	
2. NEW PROGRAMS—MINIMUM ASSISTANCE						
a. Pay as you grow	170,000	—	600	102	—	0
Rental	170,000	—	450	76.5	255	1,500
Elderly condominium	60,000	—	300	18	180	3,000
b. Section 235	40,000	—	900	36	360	9,000
Section 236	40,000	—	900	36	1,000	25,000
c. Assistance						
Public housing	—	—	—	60	2,400	
Private housing	—	120,000	500	60	2,400	20,000
	480,000	120,000		$388.5	$ 6,595	

64

Table 9 (continued)

ESTIMATED COSTS OF ALTERNATIVE HOUSING BUDGETS[a]

	No. of Units Produced	No. of Additional Households Assisted	1st Year Cost/Unit	1st Year Cost (millions)	Total Cost[b] (millions)	Per Unit Total
3. NEW PROGRAMS—MAXIMUM ASSISTANCE						
a. Pay as you grow	170,000	—	600	102	—	0
Rental	170,000	—	450	76.5	255	1,500
Elderly condominium	60,000	—	300	18	180	3,000
b. Section 235	40,000	—	900	36	360	9,000
Section 236	40,000	—	900	36	1,000	25,000
c. Assistance						
Public housing	—	—	—	60	2,400	
Private housing	—	1,000,000	500	500	20,000	20,000
	480,000	1,000,000		$828.5	$24,195	

a Cost estimates are not discounted.

b The total cost reflects a subsidy period of 40 years for the assistance elements (public housing, rent supplements and operating subsidies, plus assistance) of the three budgets.

committees have concluded that $315 million is the minimum required. An assumption of $300 million is made for this item.[6] The first-year cost of this hypothetical budget is $864 million, and the life-of-the-program cost is $27.7 billion.

New Programs in an Old Budget. Under the alternative "minimum" budget, the same number of additional households would be assisted. The mix of programs, however, would be very different. No funds would be allocated to production for the poor––that is, to develop new public housing units (whether produced conventionally, privately, or through the leasing program) or rent supplement units. These programs accounted for 120,000 units in the first budget. The interest subsidy programs would be cut back from 360,000 to 80,000 units, evenly divided between Section 235 and Section 236.

The 400,000 "lost" units would be replaced by 400,000 units subsidized under the proposed consumer-oriented production programs. Based on past allocations, a reasonable division of the units among sales, rental, and elderly would be 170,000 sales units, 170,000 rental units, and 60,000 units under the elderly condominium plan. Using per-unit costs for the sales and rental programs of $600 and $450 respectively (approximately three-quarters of the maximum amount projected in Chapter III), $300 for the condominium plan, and $900 for the interest subsidy programs, the first-year bill for the 480,000 units in question would be $268.5 million. Estimated savings over the cost of the same number of units provided under existing programs would be $295.5 million for the first year and $13.9 billion over the life of the program.

Savings would also accrue on the assistance side from the redirection of operating subsidies from LHAs to tenants. The LHAs would be allowed full discretion in setting rents. However, if a unit's rent were increased, the tenant would become eligible for the new assistance program. He would be given the choice of staying in the public unit or seeking accommodation in the private market. In either event, his rent and the federal subsidy would be determined in the same manner—that is, on the basis of income, family size, and the full rent of the unit. If the tenant chose a private unit, his subsidy payment would be continued and the LHA would choose a new tenant for its unit. The new tenant's rent and the government subsidy would be determined under the new system.

If we assume that rents rose and tenants stayed in 250,000 of the public housing units (approximately one-fourth of the LHA inventory), the $300 million operating subsidy could be cut to $60 million. The $60 million reflects a $200 per-unit subsidy, plus a $10 million Murphy-law factor. This cost projection is based on the following:

(1) The public housing crisis at present, although covering most of the major LHAs, only affects a minority of the units (approximately 300,000).[7]

(2) The median income of public housing tenants is surprisingly high, substantially above the poverty level in some regions.[8]

(3) The bulk of the LHA units had a market rent in 1969 of approximately $100 per month.

(4) The LHAs will be able to sell losing projects.

The savings that would be produced on the assistance side are estimated at $180 million the first year and $7.2 million for the life of the program.

The combined savings that would arise from redirecting both production programs and operating subsidies as summarized in the "minimum" budget would equal $475.5 million for the initial year and $21 billion over the life of the programs. This suggests a political question: how should these savings be shared between those in need of assistance and the taxpayers? Under the "minimum" budget, the number of additional households served would be held at 120,000 and the substantial savings could be passed on to the tax-paying public. Under the "maximum" budget, using an average subsidy of $500 per family, nine times more poor households could be assisted than under present programs at roughly the same total cost.

In brief, the "minimum" assistance budget would accomplish the production and assistance results of existing programs at a fraction of their cost. The "maximum" assistance budget would greatly expand the number of additional households assisted with smaller reductions in cost.

Vicious Cycles or Virtuous Circles?

An attempt to reach the national housing goal by reliance solely on production stimulus through consumer demand or solely on the assistance approach is, as a practical matter, impossible. The thirty-five year history of housing subsidy programs shows that by attempting too much, too little is produced. Existing production programs, by striving to produce large numbers of new housing units for the poor, have managed to antagonize a substantial segment of the population. To redress their grievances, those antagonized worked changes that crippled the programs' capacity to produce many units or to help many of the poor. In each case, the expectations of the poor are disappointed and new legislation is demanded, which starts the vicious cycle in motion again.

The approach suggested in this paper relies on both housing production and housing assistance programs, but it separates subsidies to bring about new production and subsidies to households unable to pay for decent housing. By separating these strategies, political interests could be brought into close harmony and a more efficient system could be created. The result might even be called a virtuous circle. Housing production programs that made the cost of new housing attractive to middle-income families would have obvious appeal in a predominantly middle-income society. The large volume of new production could also provide substantial benefits to lower-income families by allowing good used housing to flow down to them through the filtering process. This in turn would make housing assistance to the poor more attractive politically and more feasible economically—thereby, one may hope, achieving the goal of a decent home for all American families.

APPENDIX

How the Assistance Subsidy Would Work

The proposed assistance program starts with a subsidy schedule based on two factors, household size and the rent/income ratio. This appendix suggests how the subsidy schedule would be applied in specific cases.

The subsidy calculation under the assistance program relies upon elementary arithmetic. Given the size of the family, the household's income and the market rent of the unit, the subsequent task of finding the subsidy, the tenant contribution and the tenant rent/income ratio is about as difficult as finding a telephone number knowing the city, the correct spelling of the last name and the first name.

An illustration of how a page in the subsidy directory would be created shows the simplicity of the process. The subsidy scheme calls for a different level of subsidy to households of different sizes depending on their rent/income ratios. The first two columns of the directory section dealing with four-person households would show rent/income figures and subsidies. The third column on the page would show the tenant contribution required at the various rent/income ratios. Since the contribution would differ if income differed, a separate sheet would be required for fixed dollar intervals. The page applicable to a four-person household with an income of $3,100 would look as follows (figures for illustrative purposes only):

Four-Person Household—$3,100 Income

Rent/ Income Ratios	(1) Subsidy +	(2) Tenant Share =	(3) Market Rent
14%	$ 0	$434	$ 434
15	175	465	640
16	245	496	741
17	315	527	842
18	385	558	943
19	455	589	1,044
20	525	620	1,145
21	560	651	1,211
22	595	682	1,277
23	630	713	1,343
24	665	744	1,409
25	700	775	1,475
26	718	806	1,524
27	735	837	1,572
28	753	868	1,621
29	770	899	1,669
30	788	930	1,718
31	800	961	1,761
32	800	992	1,792

The table illustrates how the addition of the subsidy and tenant share meets the market rent. This reverses the usual situation in which programs start with the rent (and household size and income) and what remains to be determined is the subsidy and the tenant share. Going back to the table and using as an example a rent of $1,080 (the median annual market rent paid by the poor in low-income areas of New York City), the subsidy and tenant share for a four-person household with a $3,100 income would be determined by finding the number closest to $1,080 in the rent column and reading to the left. In the example, the subsidy and tenant share (rounding off to the nearest percentage of rent to income, 19 percent) would be $455 and $589, respectively.

NOTES

NOTES TO CHAPTER I

[1] Housing Act of 1949, Section 2, 42 U.S.C. Section 1441 (1964).

[2] As used in this monograph, an assistance strategy denotes one intended to enable poor households to pay for decent housing. It does not denote the manner in which a subsidy is delivered. For example, the current rent supplement program assists poor families even though the subsidy payment is made to the landlord.

[3] U.S. Bureau of the Census, *General Housing Characteristics—United States Summary* (Washington: U.S. Government Printing Office, 1971), Table 1.

[4] Ibid., Table 2. The statistics include vacant as well as occupied units. The vacancy rate was 10.1 percent (1,778,848 units) in rural areas and 4.9 percent (2,427,971 units) in urban areas. Ibid., Table 10. Approximately 97 percent of the urban vacant units and 88 percent of the rural vacant units were adequate. U.S. Bureau of the Census, *Current Housing Reports—Housing Vacancies* (Washington: U.S. Government Printing Office, August 1972), Table 7 (data for vacant units inside and outside of S.M.S.A.'s). There are, therefore, 1,626,843 occupied inadequate urban units (3.4 percent) and 2,772,077 occupied inadequate rural units (17.4 percent).

[5] Ibid., Table 4.

[6] Ibid.

[7] *Message from the President of the United States, Fourth Annual Housing Report on National Housing Goals* (Washington: U.S. Government Printing Office, 1972), pp. 21-23; hereinafter cited as *Fourth Annual Report.*

[8] National Commission on Urban Problems, *Building the American City: Report to the Congress and the President of the United States* (Washington: U.S. Government Printing Office, 1968), pp. 80-82; hereinafter cited as *Douglas Commission Report.*

[9] *Fourth Annual Report*, p. 46.

[10] Homeowners, who constitute roughly two-thirds of the occupants of housing, would not be burdened by rising rents.

[11] Rent to income ratios for low-income households overstate the burden of rent since many low-income households have temporarily dropped into that category from higher income categories to which they will return, particularly in a period of cyclical downturn such as 1970. See George J. Stigler, *The Theory of Price* (New York: The Macmillan Company, 1966), pp. 35-38; Milton Friedman,

A Theory of the Consumption Function (New York: National Bureau of Economic Research, 1957).

[12] U.S. Bureau of the Census, *Population & Housing Characteristics for the United States, by State 1970* (Washington: U.S. Government Printing Office, 1972), Table H-2.

[13] The level for 1973 is $4,200.

[14] See, for example, statements of Senator Long and and Senator Ribicoff during Senate debate on the "Social Security Amendments of 1972," *Congressional Record,* vol. 118, pp. S 16238-16248.

[15] James Tobin, "On Limiting the Domain of Inequality," *Journal of Law and Economics,* vol. 13 (October 1970), p. 263.

[16] Roger Scott, "Avarice, Altruism and Second Party Preferences," *The Quarterly Journal of Economics,* vol. 86 (February 1972), p. 17.

NOTES TO CHAPTER II

[1] United States Housing Act of 1937, as amended, 42 U.S.C. Section 1401 et seq.

[2] U.S. Department of Housing and Urban Development, *1971 HUD Statistical Yearbook,* Table 149 (Washington: U.S. Government Printing Office, 1971). The 947,000 unit figure does not include approximately 45,000 units that are under the Section 23 leasing program (without rehabilitation).

[3] For a more detailed calculation of the subsidy, see Irving H. Welfeld, "A New Framework for Federal Housing Aid," *Columbia Law Review,* December 1969, pp. 1361-1366.

[4] Albert Walsh, "Is Public Housing Headed for a Fiscal Crisis?" in *Journal of Housing,* February 1969, p. 65.

[5] U.S. Congress, House, Committee on Appropriations, *Hearings on the Independent Offices and HUD Appropriations, 1970, Before a Subcommittee of the House Committee on Appropriations,* 91st. Cong., 1st sess. pt. 4, p. 57 (1969).

[6] "The Distribution of Federally Assisted Rental Housing Services by Regions and States," in *The Economics of Federal Subsidy Programs,* Part 5 (Housing Subsidies), a compendium of papers submitted to the Joint Economic Committee, U.S. Congress (Washington: Government Printing Office, October 9, 1972).

[7] Richard F. Muth, *Public Housing: An Economic Evaluation* (Washington: American Enterprise Institute for Public Policy Research, 1973).

[8] U.S. Department of Housing and Urban Development, *Hearings on HUD-Space-Science-Veterans Appropriations for 1973 Before the House Committee on Appropriations* (Washington: U.S. Government Printing Office, 1972); hereinafter cited as *1973 HUD Appropriations Hearings.*

[9] "The Pathology of Public Housing," *City,* Fall 1971, p. 32.

[10] Housing and Urban Development Act of 1965, Section 101, 12 U.S.C. 1701 s.

[11] See Irving H. Welfeld, "Rent Supplements and the Subsidy Dilemma—The Equity of a Selective Subsidy System," *Law and Contemporary Problems,* vol. 32 (1967), p. 465.

[12] *Fourth Annual Report,* p. 46.

[13] National Housing Act, Section 235, 12 U.S.C. 1715 z.

[14] *Fourth Annual Report,* p. 46.

[15] Anthony Downs, *Summary Report, Federal Housing Subsidies: Their Nature and Effectiveness and What We Should Do About Them* (Chicago: Real Estate Research Corporation, October 1972).

[16] U.S. Department of Housing and Urban Development, Division of Research and Statistics, "Characteristics of Home Mortgage Transactions Insured by FHA Under Section 235(i)," Second Quarter, 1972, p. 2 (unpublished analysis); hereinafter cited as *HUD Section 235 Statistics.*

[17] Ibid., Table 1.

[18] *1973 HUD Appropriations Hearings,* p. 203.

[19] This amount is higher than HUD's estimated total cost of $7,600. The HUD figures do not include the cost of the tandem plan in which the Government National Mortgage Association purchases FHA insured Section 235 mortgages with interest rates of 7 percent at par and then sells the mortgage so that the interest rate yield is at the market which in early 1973 was between 7½ and 7¾ percent. GNMA does this by receiving only approximately ninety-five cents on the dollar and absorbing the loss by using funds supplied by the U.S. Treasury. On an $18,000 mortgage this is an additional $900 in subsidy. The HUD estimate also assumes that the original owner will not sell to a household that qualifies for the subsidy. HUD's maximum contractual obligation is $26,000. Ibid., p. 109.

[20] Wallace Smith, *Housing—The Social and Economic Element* (Berkeley, Calif.: University of California Press, 1970), p. 483.

[21] *HUD Section 235 Statistics,* p. 1.

[22] There is also a substantial advantage to the bureaucracy in this arrangement since the most effective attacks against the program come from "photogenic journalism." Thus, most of the "scandals" involving HUD housing programs relate to the hole in the ceiling and the faulty plumbing of the old and cheaper inner city unit. One of the spoken assumptions of the program is that "quality is remembered long after cost is forgotten."

[23] U.S. Congress, Senate, Committee on Banking, Housing and Urban Affairs, *Hearings on the Housing and Urban Development Act of 1970 Before the Subcommittee on Housing and Urban Affairs,* Part 1. (Washington: Government Printing Office, 1970), p. 76; hereinafter cited as *1970 Hearings.*

[24] U.S. Department of Housing and Urban Development, Division of Research and Statistics, "Insurance Written As Of December 1972" (unpublished, undated computer run).

[25] Thirty-nine percent of the families entering the program in the second quarter of 1972 had three or less persons. Twenty-one percent of the families were four-person families. *HUD Section 235 Statistics,* Table 5.

[26] Ibid., p. 2.

[27] U.S. Bureau of the Census, *1971 Housing Summary,* Table 1.

[28] See Comptroller General, *Report to the Congress—Opportunities To Improve Effectiveness and Reduce Costs of Homeownership Assistance Programs* (December 1972).

[29] U.S. Congress, Senate, Committee on Banking, Housing and Urban Affairs, *Hearings on the 1971 Housing and Urban Development Legislation Before the Subcommittee on Housing and Urban Affairs,* Part 2 (Washington: U.S. Government Printing Office, 1971), p. 857.

[30] Speech before the Meeting of the Board of Directors of the National Association of Homebuilders, October 9, 1972, pp. 35-36 (unpublished and unedited transcript from a tape recording).

[31] National Housing Act, Section 236, 12 U.S.C. 1715 z-1.

[32] *Fourth Annual Report,* p. 46.

[33] *1970 Hearings,* p. 80.

[34] See *Federal Register,* vol. 37 (June 13, 1972), p. 11758.

[35] HUD's estimated total cost is $15,200. The maximum contractual obligation is $35,100. See *1973 HUD Appropriations Hearings,* p. 109.

[36] S. 3248 Title I, Section 502, 92nd Congress, 2nd session.

[37] On the general question of why and how Section 236 is so different from the rent supplement program, see Welfeld, "That Housing Problem—The American vs. the European Experience," *Public Interest*, Spring 1972, pp. 81-85.

[38] *U.S. Treasury Department Tax Reform Studies and Proposals, Joint Publication of the House Committee on Ways and Means and the Senate on Finance*, Part 3 (Washington: U.S. Government Printing Office, 1969), pp. 438-439.

[39] Letter concerning a Section 236 project in Brockton, Massachusetts.

[40] Downs, *Federal Housing Subsidies*.

[41] Ibid., p. 20.

[42] Ibid., p. 46.

[43] Ibid.

[44] *Douglas Commission Report*, p. 130.

[45] *Hearings on Equal Educational Opportunity Before the Senate Select Commission on Equal Educational Opportunity*, Part 5 (Washington: Government Printing Office, 1971) p. 2973.

[46] Downs, *Federal Housing Subsidies*, p. 44.

[47] Ibid., p. 45.

[48] Ibid., p. 46.

[49] It is on this point that economists quarrel with the use of housing subsidies to supplement the income of the poor instead of cash grants. They suggest that the poor who are provided with housing might prefer to use some of the resources diverted to that housing for other things. To this extent, the poor would prefer a smaller cash grant to the larger amount spent on providing them with housing. See Richard Muth, *Public Housing*, Chapter II.

NOTES TO CHAPTER III

[1] See Irving H. Welfeld, *European Housing Subsidy Systems* (Washington: U.S. Government Printing Office, 1972), pp. 30-38.

[2] What would happen to the small minority of families whose incomes did not rise quickly to cover rising amortization payments? These families would not lose their homes. If the family certified that the payment would exceed 25 percent of its income (and provided evidence of its income and assets), the amortization level would be frozen. To ensure that this hardship provision would not become an excuse for sloppy underwriting, all administrative costs with respect to the provision would be borne by the lender.

[3] The median value of owner-occupied units with husband-wife families, with family head 65 years or over was $14,170 in 1969. See U.S. Department of Housing and Urban Development, *1971 White House Conference on Aging-Housing* (Washington: U.S. Government Printing Office, 1971), Table 5. Eighty-five percent of the elderly own their homes debt free.

NOTES TO CHAPTER IV

[1] 1970 Census of Population, *General Social and Economic Characteristics, United States Summary* (Washington: U.S. Government Printing Office), Table 106.

[2] The major housing allowance proposals currently under consideration are based on the "housing gap" approach.

[3] *The Report of the President's Commission on Urban Housing—A Decent Home* (Washington: Government Printing Office, 1968), pp. 62-63.

[4] *A Standard Rent Setting System for Public Housing* (unpublished draft report, February 1972), p. 2.

NOTES TO CHAPTER V

[1] Although this study has touched on the attractiveness of the proposed programs to the public as voters and taxpayers, no attempt is made to deal with its acceptability to the scores of groups that have a special and often vested interest in housing. That is a subject for another study.

[2] The budgets presented in this section are prototypes. The shifting of gears by the government as it changes program directions or program vehicles is a laborious and lengthy process. The specific budgets and program proposals presented are not meant to be prescriptions for 1973.

[3] *1973 HUD Appropriations Hearings*, p. 151. Total unit reservations in fiscal 1971 were 412,000 and in fiscal 1972, 580,000.

[4] Ibid.

[5] U.S. Congress, House, Committee on Appropriations, *Hearings on HUD-Space-Science-Veterans Appropriations for 1974 Before the House Committee on Appropriations* (Washington: U.S. Government Printing Office, 1973), p. 48.

[6] *Senate Report 272*, 93rd Congress, 1st Session, pp. 9-10.

[7] *1973 HUD Appropriations Hearings*, p. 1302.

[8] U.S. Department of Housing and Urban Development, Office of Housing Management Statistics Branch, *Families in Low-Rent Projects—Families Reexamined for Continued Occupancy, October 1, 1970-September 30, 1971* (Washington: U.S. Government Printing Office, 1972), p. 25.

Cover and book design: Pat Taylor

SELECTED 1973 PUBLICATIONS

ELECTIONS IN SOUTH VIETNAM, Howard R. Penniman (246 pages, cloth $7.50, paper $3.50)

U.S. IMPORT QUOTAS: COSTS AND CONSEQUENCES, Ilse Mintz (85 pages, $3.00)

PUBLIC HOUSING: AN ECONOMIC EVALUATION, Richard F. Muth (61 pages, $3.00)

INCREASING THE SUPPLY OF MEDICAL PERSONNEL, Charles T. Stewart, Jr., and Corazon M. Siddayao (81 pages, $3.00)

MATCHING NEEDS AND RESOURCES: REFORMING THE FEDERAL BUDGET, Murray L. Weidenbaum, Dan Larkins, and Philip N. Marcus (114 pages, $3.00)

STRUCTURAL REFORM OF THE FEDERAL BUDGET PROCESS, William A. Niskanen, Jr. (60 pages, $2.50)

DEATH AND TAXES: SOME PERSPECTIVES ON INHERITANCE, INEQUALITY, AND PROGRESSIVE TAXATION, Richard E. Wagner (63 pages, $2.50)

TAX LOOPHOLES: THE LEGEND AND THE REALITY, Roger A. Freeman (91 pages, $3.00)

FARM COMMODITY PROGRAMS: AN OPPORTUNITY FOR CHANGE, D. Gale Johnson (114 pages, $3.00)

SECTIONS 235 AND 236: AN ECONOMIC EVALUATION OF HUD'S PRINCIPAL HOUSING SUBSIDY PROGRAMS, Harrison G. Wehner, Jr. (46 pages, $2.50)

THE CHANGING FACE OF HONG KONG: NEW DEPARTURES IN PUBLIC POLICY, Alvin Rabushka (79 pages, $3.00)

POVERTY AND PUBLIC POLICY: WHAT SHOULD BE THE ROLE OF THE FEDERAL GOVERNMENT IN EXTENDING PUBLIC ASSISTANCE TO ALL AMERICANS LIVING IN POVERTY? (119 pages, $3.00)

HOW FULL IS FULL EMPLOYMENT? AND OTHER ESSAYS ON INTERPRETING THE UNEMPLOYMENT STATISTICS, Geoffrey H. Moore (32 pages, $2.00)

THE MARKET CONCENTRATION DOCTRINE: AN EXAMINATION OF EVIDENCE AND A DISCUSSION OF POLICY, Harold Demsetz (30 pages, $2.00)

RATIONALE FOR NATO: EUROPEAN COLLECTIVE SECURITY—PAST AND FUTURE, Morton A. Kaplan (94 pages, $3.00)

THE FEDERAL GOVERNMENT AND MANPOWER: A CRITICAL LOOK AT THE MDTA-INSTITUTIONAL AND JOB CORPS PROGRAMS, Dave M. O'Neill (65 pages, $3.00)

VIETNAM SETTLEMENT: WHY 1972, NOT 1969? Part I, Abram Chayes and Morton A. Kaplan; *Part II*, Paul C. Warnke and G. Warren Nutter; *Part III*, John P. Roche and Clayton Fritchey (208 pages, $5.75)

MAJOR TAX REFORM: URGENT NECESSITY OR NOT? Charls E. Walker and Henry S. Reuss (78 pages, $5.75)

ACADEMICS, POLITICS, AND THE 1972 ELECTION, Everett Carll Ladd, Jr., and Seymour Martin Lipset (99 pages, $3.00)

CAN CONGRESS CONTROL SPENDING? William Proxmire, Al Ullman, John W. Byrnes, Paul W. McCracken and Charles L. Schultz (62 pages, cloth $5.00, paper $2.50)

A NEW LOOK AT INFLATION: ECONOMIC POLICY IN THE EARLY 1970s, Phillip Cagan, Marten Estey, William Fellner, Gottfried Haberler and Charles E. McLure, Jr. (172 pages, cloth $8.50, paper $3.75)

THE EMERGENCE OF BANGLADESH: PROBLEMS AND OPPORTUNITIES FOR A REDEFINED AMERICAN POLICY IN SOUTH ASIA, Wayne Wilcox (79 pages, $3.00)

AMERICA'S HOUSING PROBLEM: AN APPROACH TO ITS SOLUTION, Irving Welfeld (75 pages, $3.00)

Discounts: 25 to 99 copies—20%; 100 to 299 copies—30%
300 to 499 copies—40%; 500 and over—50%

AMERICA'S HOUSING PROBLEM: An Approach to Its Solution by Irving Welfeld presents criteria for evaluating federal programs for housing production and housing assistance, measures these programs against the criteria, and discusses an alternative set of programs. The latter, he concludes, would achieve far better results than the existing efforts. As an example, his comparisons show that, by shifting to the proposed alternatives, the same number of new units could be constructed and nine times more poor households could be assisted at no increase in cost.

"Mr. Welfeld's monograph . . . makes a major contribution to solving the problems posed by our housing programs." GEORGE ROMNEY, former Secretary of Housing and Urban Development. "An excellent study whose approach is thoughtful, and also new— which is no small distinction in territory which most others cross only over deeply rutted paths. . . . My own way of viewing the terrain will never be the same again." HILBERT FEFFERMAN, associate general counsel for legislation, Department of Housing and Urban Development (1966-73).

Irving Welfeld, an analyst in the Department of Housing and Urban Development and formerly an attorney in the Office of General Counsel there, is a graduate of the Harvard Law School. He is the author of a government monograph entitled "European Housing Subsidy Systems—An American Perspective," as well as articles that have appeared in law journals and in The Public Interest.

$3.00

 American Enterprise Institute for Public Policy Research
1150 Seventeenth Street, N.W., Washington, D. C. 20036